Without Precedent

Without Precedent

Scripture, Tradition, and the Ordination of Women

Geoffrey Kirk

WIPF & STOCK · Eugene, Oregon

WITHOUT PRECEDENT
Scripture, Tradition, and the Ordination of Women

Wipf & Stock
An Imprint of Wipf and Stock Publishers
199 W. 8th Ave., Suite 3
Eugene, OR 97401

www.wipfandstock.com

PAPERBACK ISBN: 978-1-4982-3081-0
HARDCOVER ISBN: 978-1-4982-3083-4

Manufactured in the U.S.A.

In piam memoriam

A M F

Contents

Acknowledgements | ix

Introduction | xi

1: Truth and Principle | 1

2: What did Jesus Really Think about Women? | 27

3: Gentiles, Slaves, and Women | 48

4: Alas, Poor Andronicus! | 66

5: Magdalena Apostola? | 78

6: Mosaics, Catacombs and Concelebrations | 96

7: Conclusions | 115

Bibliography | 137

Subject Index | 151

Scripture Index | 159

Acknowledgements

B ooks begin with conversations. I owe a debt of gratitude first to Jenny Standage. The conversations with Jenny—in a curious but rewarding friendship between the National Secretaries of the Movement for the Ordination of Women and of Forward in Faith—have lasted for two decades and are not over. Neither party, I think, would claim to have changed minds in any fundamental way; but despite the surrounding political heat, light has been generated.

I am also grateful to the clergy and people of the Most Precious Blood, SE1, who have shared parts of what follows and offered me comments and reflections. I especially thank Joanna Bogle and Antonia Lynn.

It was Dr. Colin Podmore who first encouraged me to write. His generosity with his time and the wisdom of his contributions to the conversation have been an inspiration. He worked tirelessly in helping prepare the text for publication, and rescued me from numerous errors and inaccuracies. Needless to say, the errors that remain are mine alone.

Introduction

I had thought to begin this introduction with an apology. Over twenty years on from the first ordinations of women priests in the Church of England, and over half a century since the debate began in earnest, yet another book on the subject might be thought to be trying the public's patience. But apology, it turns out, would be superfluous: there are so few books.

In his invaluable collection of essays, "Aspects of Anglican Identity,"[1] Dr. Colin Podmore provides a useful summary of the discussion documents related to the synodical process in the Church of England. These slender volumes begin with the report, "Women in Holy Orders."[2] In 1968, the Anglican Consultative Council (a very different organization in those days) issued a discussion document, "Women in Ministry: A Study,"[3] which was sent out for debate among all the Provinces of the Anglican Communion. A short time later, the Church of England's Advisory Council for the Church's Ministry published a paper entitled "The Ordination of Women to the Priesthood."[4] This was the first of a number of synodical contributions by Miss (later Dame) Christian Howard. Howard was a member of a well-known Northern family with strong connections to the suffragette movement. Though lacking any formal university education (she attended finishing schools in Italy and France), she became a significant figure in the General Synod and later became a member of the World Council of

---

1. Podmore, *Aspects of Anglican Identity*.
2. Church Information Office, *Women in Holy Orders*.
3. Advisory Council, *Women in Ministry: A Study*.
4. GS 104 [Howard], *Ordination of Women to the Priesthood*.

Churches Faith and Order Commission and its first woman vice-moderator. Her other contributions were "A Supplement"[5] and "A Further Report."[6] The first contribution of the House of Bishops of the Church of England to the unfolding debate[7] was a response to the recommendations of a synod working party on the possible shape of legislation, and only in a very limited sense a theological commentary. It was in 1988 that the House provided a more substantial (140-page) report[8] that addressed scriptural and doctrinal issues directly. Like the previous House of Bishops report, GS 829 was claimed to be "unanimous"; though in fact it revealed substantial differences of opinion within the House on almost every topic raised. The then religious affairs correspondent of *The Times*, Clifford Longley, who was present at the press launch, commented laconically that it was a very Anglican use of the term "unanimous." The next official synodical contribution to the debate was in "The Rochester Report"[9] (a substantial theological report of 289 pages, published in November 2004). It was followed by a summary in March of the same year.

Whatever one's attitude to the result of this process, there can be no doubt that it was both more thorough and more extensive than any undertaken elsewhere in the Anglican Communion. After posing several critical questions about the synodical process, Podmore concludes his overview thus:

> Whatever the answer to these questions, the Church of England can take pride in its synodical system. No one could claim that the Synod acted hastily or without due consideration. Only after 22 years of debate and discussion was a motion calling for legislation passed, and the process from then until the promulgation of the canon took more than nine further years. The legislation was prepared and revised with great care and attention to detail, and debated not only in the General and diocesan Synods but in each deanery synod. The final approval debate was widely praised for its tone and quality by those who heard a Synod debate for the first time on radio or television.[10]

---

5. GS Misc 88 [Howard], *Ordination of Women: Supplement*.

6. GS Misc 198 [Howard], *Ordination of Women: Further Report*.

7. GS 764, *Ordination of Women: First Report*.

8. GS 829, *Ordination of Women: Second Report*.

9. GS 1557, *Women Bishops in the Church of England?*

10. Podmore, *Aspects of Anglican Identity*, 133.

All well and good. But such a survey of the material, useful as it is, omits the most important feature of the debate—which is, of course, the absence of any serious contributions from the academic community. The big beasts of the theological academy are conspicuous by their absence. They seem deliberately to have avoided the subject, even when they were themselves involved in the synodical process. How might the debate have been illuminated by a pithy, incisive monograph by David Jenkins, a door-stopping assessment by Tom Wright, or a measured, ingenious, convoluted defense of the innovation by Rowan Williams? We will never know. They left the debate, for the most part, to the also-rans. Back in the mists of history, it is true there were contributions (albeit brief) of some weight. One thinks of the essay by C. S. Lewis, "Priestesses in the Church?"[11] and the short paper by Bishop Henley Henson.[12] But even so, they are few. A matter of months before his death, I asked Eric Mascall why neither he nor his contemporaries had written anything substantial on the subject. He drew my attention to the paper by V. A. Demant[13] and concluded ruefully: "I suppose we just did not see it coming."

This reluctance to enter the fray has a number of causes. The waters, it is true, were already very muddy. Absurd claims were being made by proponents (some of them detailed in this book), which any serious academic assessment would have to ignore or contest. And, in due deference to the ladies, no one really wanted to do either. But more than that, there was the overwhelming conviction of the *bien-pensants* (especially in the left-leaning academy) that this was an open and shut case. Even to argue in its favor was to demonstrate an unacceptable degree of political incorrectness. In the Church hierarchy, moreover, there was a cliquishness, which meant that this matter, like others which were deemed unstylishly contentious, had better be avoided. "His clear preference," wrote Gary Bennett of Robert Runcie, in the fateful Crockford's Preface, "is for men of liberal disposition and a moderately Catholic style which is not taken to the point of having firm principles. If in addition they have a good appearance and are articulate over the media, he is prepared to overlook a certain theological deficiency."[14] "I had to change," said Rowan Williams to Angela Tilby

11. Lewis, "Priestesses in the Church?" (Originally published as "Notes on the Way," in *Time and Tide* 29.)

12. Henson, "Ordination of Women."

13. Demant, *Why the Christian Priesthood is Male.*

14. Preface to *Crockford's Clerical Directory*, 68.

of his early objections to women's ordination, "after looking around at my side and seeing the company I was keeping."[15] The result was that the only serious theological study on the subject of women's ordination available to English readers, then and now, was an American translation of the work of a German priest published in San Francisco in 1988.[16] At a conference in St. George's College Windsor in 2000, on the then fashionable "Doctrine of Reception," I asked Dr. Mary Tanner (sometime Moderator of the World Council of Churches Faith and Order Commission and head of the Church of England's Council for Christian Unity and drafter of the 1988 Bishops' Report) her opinion of the book. She had not read it.

The widening gap between the world of academic theology and the day-to-day life of the Church which this lacuna demonstrates—and the ecclesial dominance of what Bennett called men "who have nothing to prevent them following what they think is the wish of the majority of the moment"[17]—were the real marks of this debate. The General Synod routinely congratulates itself on the quality and tone of its proceedings; but there must surely, after reading the verbatim record of November 11, 1992, be room to doubt whether such a process and such a forum is either adequate or appropriate for such a decision. It will be said that there is no other way. In the absence of prolonged and mature theological discussion, that is certainly the case.

* * *

A word of warning: This book is not an attempt to argue *against* the ordination of women to the priesthood or the episcopate, in the Church of England or in any other church. The Orders of the church are not at the disposal of Popes, Councils, synods or debating chambers of any kind. They are a gift from the Lord. We may seek to illustrate the nature and explain the purpose of that *donné*—we can seek "to justify the ways of God to man"—but we cannot properly argue for or against it, for the simple reason that it is not ours either to attack or to defend. Historically speaking, the three-fold orders of bishop, priest, and deacon emerged in their enduring form around the end of the fourth century, along with the catholic creeds and the canon of scripture. These are the three legs of the stool (not the

---

15. Shortt, *Rowan's Rule: Biography of the Archbishop*, 95.

16. Hauke, *Women in the Priesthood? Systematic Analysis.*

17. Preface to *Crockford's Clerical Directory*, 68.

trio of scripture, tradition, and reason, recently foisted on poor Hooker) on which the church sits. To alter any of them in any way is a serious and dangerous matter.

> . . . untune that string / And Hark! What discord follows; each thing meets / in mere oppugnancy.[18]

All three are now under concerted attack, not from the critics of the church, but from its own leaders. The creeds have been rendered susceptible to meanings and interpretations very far from the conceivable intention of their original drafters. The very notion of canonicity, in scripture as in other areas, has been called into question, and documents of a very different character given equivalence with the received texts. These are serious matters to which the Church of England is ill equipped to give an ecclesial response. But changes to the Orders of the church are of another dimension. Such changes objectify opinion in ecclesial structures. That is why the arguments for, and the assumptions underlying, such an innovation demand the closest possible scrutiny.

18. Shakespeare, *Troilus and Cressida*, act 1, scene 3.

1: Truth and Principle

If the first casualty of war is the unwelcome truth, the first weapon of the discontented is the welcome lie.

—PROFESSOR MICHAEL NOLAN

C hristianity is an historical religion. By that is meant not simply that like all things else it has a history; but that it is peculiarly related to a particular historical moment. Christianity relates to Christ. By that is meant not merely a notional savior (a "Christ figure" as one might say), but Jesus of Nazareth. The post-Christian theologian Daphne Hampson, in her book *Theology and Feminism*, puts the matter very clearly:

> Christians believe in particularity. That is to say they believe that God was in some sense differently related to particular events, or may be said in particular to have revealed God's self through those events, in a way in which this is not true of all other events or periods in history. Above all they believe that that must be said of Christ which is to be said of no other human being. However they may express his uniqueness, they must say of Jesus of Nazareth that there was a revelation of God through him in a way in which this is not true of you or me. God is bound up with peculiar events, a particular people, above all with the person Jesus of Nazareth. Therefore reference must needs always be made to this history and to this person.[1]

It is, of course, possible to admit the truth of that observation and still to see that there are profound problems. Who exactly is the Jesus of Nazareth to whom reference is necessarily made? What do we mean by "historical"?

1. Hampson, *Theology and Feminisim*, 8.

1

And how can we be certain that we have grasped and comprehended the import of the "historical moment"? These are not quibbles. If the aim of the Church is to base itself on the will, purpose, and intention of Jesus of Nazareth, it must have confidence in its means of discerning what that will and intention is.

What is usually called "the quest for the historical Jesus" began with Hermann Samuel Reimarus, a professor at the University of Hamburg in the mid-eighteenth century, whose thesis was so explosive that it was not published in full until 1972. For almost two hundred years the project remained a largely German undertaking, though from the late nineteenth century onwards, a few British, French, and American academics made their contributions. The aim was to identify a "human" Jesus, distinct from the divine "Christ of faith" exhibited in the Gospels and Epistles. The notion that there might be no useful distinction was not entertained. Recently when Joseph Ratzinger wrote as though they were one and the same, Geza Vermes dismissed the resulting volumes with something approaching scorn.[2] In the 1970s the action moved from Germany to England, and then, predominantly, America. It concentrated—after the discovery of the Dead Sea Scrolls—on the Jewishness of Jesus and located him in the ethos of inter-testamental and post-biblical Judaism. Two things are clear from this protracted exercise: the first, that its conclusions are tentative and precarious; the second, that it makes assumptions about the supernatural which put it at variance with the scriptural witness and with Christian belief.

At the end of the first stage of the quest, in 1906, Albert Schweitzer famously called the whole operation into question. It was, he claimed, hopelessly subjective. Each scholar, he said, merely paraded before us a Jesus of his own invention, made in his own image and likeness.[3] Equally famously, twenty years later, the great Rudolf Bultmann, the originator of *Formgeschichte*, came to an even more devastating conclusion: "We can know almost nothing about the life and personality of Jesus," he wrote, "since the early Christian sources show no interest in either."[4]

Reimarus, the originator of the Quest, was a Deist, and in many respects the inspiration of Lessing, who published fragments of his work. Both played their part in the general Enlightenment project for the reinterpretation of Christianity as a religion of humanitarian morality independent of

2. Vermes, *Searching for the Real Jesus*, 47–50.
3. Schweitzer, *Quest of the Historical Jesus*, 396–97.
4. Bultmannm, *Jesus and the Word*, 8.

all divine intervention or revelation. Integral to the Quest, from the very beginning, was the premise that an "historical," a purely "human," Jesus could not have had and could not have supposed himself to have had, a divine origin. In short, the questers ruled out the miraculous, the providential, and the supernatural—the main burden of the biblical texts—and saw those texts as merely a rich vein (alas, almost the only vein) to be mined for more mundane information. The result was to undermine the concept of canonicity, and the very authority of the texts. But that, of course, was the intention. Jesus is a fascinating character—but not obviously more so than, for example, Alexander the Great or Julius Caesar. Apart, that is, from the great prize of demolishing the pretentions of the Christian Church in the process of "rediscovery."

All this inevitably relates to the question of the ordination of women. Because of the historical nature of Christianity, reference must necessarily be made, in commending such an innovation, to the teaching of Jesus. The question on the campus t-shirts becomes the sixty-four thousand dollar question: "What would Jesus do?" But how to answer it on a subject—the social and cultic status of women—which Jesus never directly addresses? If Schweitzer was right the answers will have no more authority than the opinions of the inquirer. If Bultmann was right no conclusions will be possible at all. The feminist theologian Judith Ochshorn bravely applied to Jesus what Bultmann took to be axiomatic for the New Testament writers as a whole. "Jesus was neither a misogynist nor a feminist," she writes, "his interests simply lay elsewhere."[5] Because the question of women's ordination is necessarily being put in the context of a wider historical quest that rejects the divine origin and supernatural claims of the Jesus it strives to reveal, we need to ask what authority could its conclusions possibly have. Why should the attitudes to women of one peripatetic first century rabbi be more significant than those of another, and why should either be conclusive for us now? It would surely be absurd to seek to resolve twenty-first century issues by reference to a first century figure about whom so little can be known.

The most profound difficulty for a Christianity which seeks to be faithful to an historical moment is this problem of the miraculous. Christianity is not simply a religion which necessarily relates to past events (or to a privileged account of them); it is also a religion deeply committed to a belief in miracles. By that is meant, not merely a fascination with the remarkable and inexplicable (such as the miracles of Jesus—which, as has often been

5. Ochshorn, *Female Experience and the Divine*, 170.

noted, are comparable with those of other contemporary wonder workers, and subject to the same criteria of credibility), but a commitment to a notion of divine action and intervention, determining both the course and significance of events. Christianity is essentially teleological: "the book of life begins with a man and woman in a garden, and ends with Revelations." The dogmatic structure of the religion is crucially dependent upon the miraculous nature of the events surrounding the birth and death of Jesus. But, as anyone can see, belief in such divine interventions has been largely absent from the post-Enlightenment world and from the historiography that has developed within it. It has also markedly diminished in the mainstream Protestant churches. Churchmen of distinction have, sometimes scrupulously, sometimes flippantly, dissociated themselves from it. "I wouldn't put it past God to arrange for a virgin birth if he wanted to," said David Jenkins when he was Bishop-designate of Durham, "but I very much doubt that he would." Later, in the same television appearance, he described the Resurrection as "a series of experiences" rather than an event. These statements, of course, prove nothing about how widely such views are held. What they do show, however, is that the opinions of Voltaire and Diderot are no longer any impediment to ecclesiastical preferment.

When did the age of miracle cease? For English speakers, at least, we can be fairly accurate. It was in 1758 when the publication of David Hume's *An Enquiry Concerning Human Understanding* finally included the essay "Of Miracles," which Henry Home had advised against publishing some years before. Hume defines miracle as "a transgression of a law of nature by a particular volition of the Deity, or by the interposition of some invisible agent." He develops a notion that had originated in disputes with the learned Jesuits of the college at La Fleche in Anjou during a stay in 1735:

> . . . No testimony is sufficient to establish a miracle, unless the testimony be of a kind that its falsehood would be more miraculous than the fact which it endeavours to establish; and even in that case there is a mutual destruction of arguments and the superior only gives us an assurance suitable to that degree of force which remains after deducting the inferior.[6]

The Jesuits of La Fleche pointed out to Hume that his arguments (which had been principally directed against claims of recent miracles in their own community) were in fact arguments against the whole nature and tenor of Christianity itself. Hume tactfully moved away from the subject; but his

6. Hume, *Essays and Treatises*, vol. 2, 115–16.

interlocutors were right. The full implications of the dispute would unfold in the course of time.

The arguments of the Jesuits of La Fleche were precisely those of John Locke, whose short treatise "A Discourse of Miracles" (1701), Hume had been surprised to find in their college library. With daring circularity, Locke maintained that miraculous events give credibility to a divine messenger; and the divinity of the messenger confirms the miraculous nature of the events. Like a pair of revelers returning from a party, the two are sustained by mutual pressure: remove one and both fall into the ditch.

But the voice that caused the age of miracles to cease across the greater part of Europe was not a British voice. It was that of a deracinated Portuguese Jew from Amsterdam. Baruch (Benedict) Spinoza's attitude to miracles differs radically from that of David Hume. Hume, famously, was making an epistemological point about what a person does or does not have reason to believe. Spinoza treats the matter metaphysically. For Hume a miracle is highly unlikely, to the point of incredibility; for Spinoza, "a miracle, either contrary to or above nature, is mere absurdity." For a century or more, the name of Spinoza, and the accusation of "Spinozism," was toxic among all but the most radical Enlighteners. His "one substance" doctrine was rightly seen by the majority as the root of religious and social subversion. It involved, in the end, a denial of the possibility of hierarchies, divine or social, and heralded the triumph of a radical democracy, which was seen by many as no more than license and anarchy.

An excommunicated, deracinated Amsterdam Jew of the seventeenth century seems, at first sight, an unlikely candidate to be the inspiration of a British post-Christian feminist of the 1980s. Spinoza has little or nothing to say about the cultic status of women (or men, for that matter); it was for him, of course, a total irrelevance. But his influence is to be felt nevertheless. Two elements of Spinoza's program have especially influenced Hampson: his doctrine of miracles and his principles of scriptural exegesis.

At the same time as rejecting the miraculous, Spinoza demanded that scripture be read in precisely the manner adopted for other works of literature. Scripture, he thought, may (or may not) contain enduring ethical lessons and principles (the truth or utility of which will be determined by means other than traditional methods of exegesis); but the task of the interpreter should be restricted simply to determining, so far as possible, what the author meant to convey. Spinoza (rather wickedly) uses the reformation formula "sola scriptura" to define his position. The study of scripture "from scripture alone" means respecting the text itself, and the genius of the language in which it is written, and involving all other relevant factors, such as the social and political circumstances of its composition and the biographies of its authors. All this, which seemed outrageous in his own day, has become commonplace. Hampson takes it on board, with a clearer than usual view of its implications. Like Spinoza, she denies the very possibility of miracles (and, *a fortiori*, the incarnation and the atonement), and stresses the rootedness of the scriptural texts in the patriarchal, misogynist societies which gave them birth.

> Now I am not myself a Christian because I do not believe that there could be this particularity. I do not believe, whatever I may mean by God, that it could be said of God that God was differently related to one age or people than God is related to all ages or people. God is something which is always available, however much people in some ages, or some people in each age, may appear to be more aware of God. To put this differently and more technically, I do not believe that the causal nexus of history, or that of nature, could be broken. That is to say I do not believe that there could be peculiar events, such as a resurrection, or miracles, events which interrupt the normal causal relationships persisting in history and in nature. I do not believe in uniqueness. Thus I do not for example think that there could be a human person (which Christians must proclaim) who stood in a different relationship to God than do all other human beings[7].

At the same time, she accepts what has come to be the consensus of modern "questers": that any search for an historical Jesus will uncover a character who is embedded in the patriarchal culture of intertestamental Judaism. The Bible was written by misogynists, for misogynists.

> That the bible reflects a patriarchal world is clear. The majority of biblical figures, whether patriarchs, prophets, priests, disciples or church leaders, are male. The scriptures largely concern the interaction of men with one another and with their God. The central figure of the tradition for Christians, Jesus Christ, is of course male. A handful of women who play a part on the stage form the exception. Likewise parables and ethical sayings are largely directed to the world of men. But it is not simply that women are notable by

7. Hampson, *Theology and Feminism*, 8.

their absence. When they are present they are present for the most part performing female roles as defined by that society.[8]

Unusually for a professional theologian, Hampson goes on to relate her radical *a priori* ethical position on the equality of the sexes to the doctrine of God (or god). Her god is like the cat that walks by itself: all places, all things, and all people are alike to it. It does not—it cannot—make distinctions or have preferences. *Deus sive natura*—God as Nature—as Spinoza expressed it, is the ultimate egalitarian. Hampson reached this position in the course of arguing—in Scotland at first, and later in England—for the ordination of women. "I worked all hours, sacrificing my career and my free time, for the cause of the ordination of women in the British Anglican churches." The fruit of that work was the increasingly pressing realization that feminism (defined as a radical assertion of the equality of women and men) was incompatible with the Christian religion. How could a religion centered upon a God who became a man (worse still, a "Father" who sent his "Son")—and one whose every sacred text and whose whole history was mired in perennial patriarchy—ever concede real equality to women? Hampson had come to see that her most deeply held convictions were a reason, not to embrace women's ordination (she was at one stage an ordinand herself), but to reject Christianity.

Though described by Rowan Williams as "essential reading,"[9] Hampson's book was predictably less popular with those among whom she had labored so hard and so long. It received polite notices from hard-line feminists, but was side-lined by the rest. What Williams described as "disturbing clarity" about "the difficulties in reconciling any kind of Christian theology with feminist insights," and proposing "far-reaching re-imagining of our language about God," was less than good news to those who were still engaged in the battle for women priests and bishops. They knew that such talk was guaranteed to frighten the horses. They saved their scorn for another book appearing at much the same time and stating a similar case from an opposite position (*What will happen to God* by William Oddie).[10] *Theology and Feminism* they damned with faint praise; perhaps because it revealed, pellucidly, what the campaign for women's ordination really is—a belated and localized skirmish in the culture wars between Christianity and rationalist secularism which have been on-going since the mid-seventeenth century.

8. Ibid., 91.

9. Ibid., blurb.

10. Oddie, *What Will Happen to God?*

But Williams was right. Daphne Hampson's case is made with alarming clarity. Any critique of the arguments used to secure the ordination of women, in the British Anglican churches and in the wider church, needs to take seriously the points she makes. Hampson treated the matter—whether women should receive ordination in the Christian churches—with the utmost seriousness. It is for her a question of truth and principle. The truth is the very nature and ethical tenor of the religion; the principle is the absolute and non-negotiable equality of women and men. The two, she concludes, are radically incompatible; and as a true heir of the Enlightenment, she opts for the latter. It is a choice that Christian feminists (especially, one is tempted to say, in the cosy seclusion of the Church of England) have seldom seen the necessity of making. The problem on which Christian feminists have turned their back is that of the intellectual origins of their own movement. The "scandalous particularity" of Christianity proves, in the end, to be incompatible with a worldview that espouses radical egalitarianism. To the old riddle "How odd of God to choose the Jews," the radical egalitarian must necessarily answer that s/he didn't, or—more to the point—that s/he couldn't have. The "far-reaching re-imagining of our language about God," of which Rowan Williams spoke, turns out to require the elimination of every last vestige of Christian doctrine. Incarnation, Atonement, Final Judgement, Hell and Heaven: all must go.

* * *

Strangely but predictably, there is much in common between Hampson's radical post-Christian position and that of traditionalist opponents of women's ordination. She rejects Christianity and they reject feminism, for the same reasons. Where Hampson parts company with her forebears in the radical Enlightenment is in her understanding of what she calls "concretion": the embodiment of the essential ideas of the religion in lively and compelling images. Enlightenment thinkers were generally disposed to a reductionist view of religion. For them it was merely extravagant language about something else—something which could be simply stated and independently arrived at by rational argument. Spinoza, for example, seems to have held that the sum total of the teachings of Judaism and Christianity amounted to the rabbinical charge to love God and neighbor. The rest—the election of the Jews, the divinity of Christ—was mere persiflage. "Religion stands in no need of the trappings of superstition. On the contrary its glory is diminished when it is embellished with such fancies." Thomas Jefferson famously encouraged Joseph Priestley to compile an edition of the gospels which excised the miracles and omitted the resurrection; and when Priestley reneged on the project, he did it himself. "I have performed this operation for my own use, by cutting verse by verse out of the printed book, and arranging the matter which is evidently his, and which is as easily distinguishable as diamonds in a dunghill. The result is an octavo of forty-six pages, of pure and unsophisticated doctrines."[11]

Hampson differs. She sees that *kerygma* cannot so readily be separated from *mythos*. And rather surprisingly, she quotes C. S. Lewis approvingly to that effect:

> Suppose the reformer stops saying that a good woman may be like God and begins saying that God is like a good woman. Suppose he says that we might just as well pray to "Our Mother which art in Heaven" . . . Suppose he suggests that the Incarnation might just as well have taken a female as a male form, and the Second Person of the Trinity be as well called the Daughter as the Son. . . . But Christians think that God Himself has taught us how to speak of Him. To say that it does not matter is to say either that all the masculine imagery is not inspired, is merely human in origin, or else that, though inspired, it is quite arbitrary and unessential. And this is surely intolerable. . . . A child who had been taught to pray to a Mother in Heaven would have a religious life radically different from that of a Christian child.[12]

Hampson goes on to quote Austin Farrer, for whom the images are given in the same way.

> "As for the terms in which St. Paul expressed it—well, there you are—he used any sort of figure that came to hand: he picked up a rhetorical metaphor from a cynic preaching in the market. . . . He would have been amazed to learn that subsequent generations would make such stuff the foundation of dogmas. We should strip off the fashions of speech; but keep the substance, of course." . . . But what is the substance? It has an uncanny trick of evaporating once its accidents of expression are all removed. Now the thought of Christ Himself was expressed in certain dominant images. . . . These tremendous images . . . are not the whole of Christ's teaching, but they set forth the supernatural mystery which is the heart

11. Cappon, *Adams-Jefferson Letters*, 323.

12. Lewis, "Priestesses in the Church?"

of the teaching. . . . It is because the spiritual instruction is related to the great images, that it becomes revealed truth. . . . We have to listen to the Spirit speaking divine things: and the way to appreciate his speech is to quicken our own minds with the life of the inspired images. . . . Theology is the analysis and criticism of the revealed images. . . . Theology tests and determines the sense of the images, it does not create it. The images, of themselves, signify and reveal.[13]

Those familiar with his work will know that Farrer expands the same point, with characteristic depth of perception, in his English appreciation of Bultmann.

There are certain steps in demythicization which, being the elimination of puerile error, can be got through once for all and not repeated, but there is another sort of demythicization which never ends in this life because it belongs to the very form of our religious thought. When we pray, we must begin by conceiving God in full and vigorous images, but we must go on to acknowledge the inadequacy of them and to adhere nakedly to the imageless truth of God. The crucifixion of the images in which God is first shown to us is a necessity of prayer because it is a necessity of life. The promise of God's dealing with us through grace can be set before us in nothing but images, for we have not yet experienced the reality. When we proceed to live the promises out, the images are crucified by the reality, slowly and progressively, never completely, and not always without pain: yet the reality is better than the images. Jesus Christ clothed himself in all the images of messianic promise, and in living them out, crucified them: but the crucified reality is better than the figures of prophecy. This is very God and life eternal, whereby the children of God are delivered from idols.[14]

For Farrer, as for Hampson, what is conveyed is certainly not identical with, but nevertheless is clearly shaped by, the concretion. Christ, fulfilling the archetypal images, is both King and Victim. But he is not less a king because he is a victim; for the Cross is the consummation of his reign. "Concretion," Farrer is saying, is effected, not merely by *employing* the images; but by *living and fulfilling* them. Which is precisely what Jesus did and the Christian is called to do. It is the tragedy of the arguments in favor of women's ordination that they have sloganized Galatians 3:28 and paid so

13. Farrer, *Glass of Vision*, 37–38, 42–43, 44.

14. Bartsch and Fuller, *Kerygma and Myth*, 222–23.

little attention to the fifth chapter of the letter to the Ephesians. There, Paul portrays the marital bond as an acted parable of the divine love—of Christ's love for the Church. Only when the imagery is put into action is its truth experienced and known. The existential reality is both sweeter and more bitter than the images of prophecy.

A similar idea is developed in *Inter Insigniores*, the declaration of the Sacred Congregation for the Doctrine of the Faith on the question of the admission of women to the ministerial priesthood, which was approved by Pope Paul VI on October 15, 1976 (less than a month after the General Convention of the Episcopal Church in the USA approved the ordination of women to the priesthood and episcopate).

> [The incarnation] cannot be disassociated from the economy of salvation; it is, indeed, in harmony with the entirety of God's plan . . . For the salvation offered by God to men and women . . . took on, from the Old Testament Prophets onwards, the privileged form of a nuptial mystery: for God the Chosen People is seen as his ardently loved spouse. . . . Christ is the Bridegroom; the Church is his bride, whom he loves because he has gained her by his blood.[15]

And traditionalists have made a related point by reminding exegetes that scripture is, to a large extent, narrative. It is itself a parable. That the principal protagonists in the tale are male cannot be said to be insignificant. Different protagonists, after all, would mean a different story.

> The matter can be put succinctly: is it remotely imaginable that the foundational "story" of Christian tradition could revolve around a female savior, crucified on Calvary? Surely, whatever might be involved in such an event, it would be something quite different from the death of Jesus Christ. His sacrificial death not only fulfills the scriptural pattern (looking back to Joseph, to Isaac and, reaching back even beyond the inauguration of the covenant with Abraham, to Abel), it also resonates with human instinct and human experience in general.[16]

Hampson agrees:

> Consider then the following. A book, edited by Hans-Ruedi Weber (until recently of the World Council of Churches), On a Friday Noon, shows illustrations of Christ crucified, drawn from all cultures and times in history. The variety is fascinating. There

15. Sacred Congregation, *Inter Insigniores*, para. 2.
16. Baker, *Consecrated Women*, 14.

are yellow Christs and brown Christs, Christs who are serene and Christs in agony, Christs who are stylized and Christ in the image of the people who depicted him. But one thing these pictures— which reflect a spectrum of human art and imagination—have in common: they are all images of a man. If there were to be an image of a woman in that book, that one picture would stand out as the exception. However Christ is understood, as people take him up into their culture, or make of him what they will, they know him to be male. A woman is the "opposite" to Christ in a way in which someone of another race is not.[17]

The observation is simple and telling. Sex, says Hampson, is the great "cutting" of mankind (the Latin root means "to cut," as in "section" and "secateurs"). It transcends cultural and racial boundaries and is deeply rooted in the facts of procreation. It is this common experience of sexual difference, located in biology and rich in cultural and literary associations, which allows the myth of Oedipus, for example, to speak to a nineteenth century bourgeois Jewish consulting-room in Vienna as well as in the furthest recesses of Hellenic history. Christian feminists often feel obliged to claim that the sex of Jesus is no more "soteriologically significant" than his Jewishness. The overwhelming evidence of human experience in every culture indicates otherwise.

This fundamental agreement between a post-Christian feminist and a catholic traditionalist—between Daphne Hampson and Austin Farrer—issues, of course, in the paradox of compulsion and expulsion. What drives her from Christianity is what he finds most compelling in it. At the same time, the common ground between them defines the task for those feminists who, for whatever reason, opt to remain in the Church. They cannot reject the miraculous and providential elements of the religion like Hampson; nor can they embrace and celebrate them, like Farrer. Instead they need somehow to demonstrate that what is providential is nevertheless inconsequential. And that is a tall order. They have attempted this in two ways. Either they have sought to minimize the significance of the "maleness" of the incarnation, or they have supposed that women's ordination will in some way correct a current "imbalance" in religious imagery—will initiate a new "concretion," as one might put it.

* * *

17. Hampson, *Theology and Feminism*, 77

The first line of argument, seeking to minimize the "maleness" of Jesus, was starkly set out in a pamphlet published in England for the Movement for the Ordination of Women in 1990. It concluded with the sweeping statement: "that the risen and ascended Jesus has no gender." Jesus was a boy child; but in heaven he has no sex. This ploy of locating the necessarily genderless Jesus in a cosmic Christ beyond the grave might at first seem ingenious. It even gains some support from a saying of Jesus himself about the risen life (Mark 12:25). But only a moment's reflection is required to see that it is clear contrary to the Christian doctrine of the resurrection, which hangs upon the identification between the earthly and the risen body of the Savior—a doctrine familiar to every worshipper from Wesley's splendid Advent hymn:

> Those dear tokens of his passion
> Still his dazzling body bears
> cause of endless exaltation
> to his ransomed worshippers.
> With what rapture gaze we on those glorious scars.[18]

What, we are entitled to ask, would a forensic pathologist make of a human body with identifiable scar tissue but no indicators of the sex of the deceased?

Dr. Susannah Cornwall, a research fellow at Manchester University's Lincoln Theological Institute, has boldly gone where no scholarship has gone before. In an article entitled "Intersex & Ontology: A Response to 'The Church, Women Bishops and Provision,'" she is responding to a theological paper produced by the Evangelical think-tank The Latimer Trust. That Jesus was male, she claims, is "simply a best guess." It is impossible to know "with any certainty," she says, that Jesus did not have both male and female organs.

> There is no way of knowing for sure that Jesus did not have one of the intersex conditions which would give him a body which appeared externally to be unremarkably male, but which might nonetheless have had some "hidden" female physical features . . . There is simply no way of telling at this juncture whether Jesus was an unremarkably male human being, or someone with an intersex condition who had a male morphology as far as the eye could see but may or may not also have had XX chromosomes or some

18. John and Charles Wesley (1758), adapted from John Cennick (1752), revised by Martin Madan (1760).

female internal anatomy. The fact that, as far as we know, Jesus never married, fathered children or engaged in sexual intercourse, of course, makes his "undisputable" maleness even less certain.[19]

But this uncertainty has, for Cornwall, some very certain consequences. It deprives the terms male and female, man and woman, of any useful content—so eliminating at a stroke the subject matter of the greater part of world literature. Nothing and no one can any more be manly or womanly. Cornwall's claim, of course, is one which could be made, on the self-same grounds—that is, none at all—about every historical personage from Socrates to Adolf Hitler. I have not chosen these names entirely at random. Both might be thought to be a more fruitful subject for speculation than Jesus of Nazareth: with Socrates there are the accusations of corrupting youth; and with Hitler the familiar words to the tune of "Colonel Bogey."

These rather ham-fisted attempts to geld Christianity's Lord have probably been influenced by the American Episcopalian patristics scholar Richard A. Norris Jr. Norris, it need hardly be said, is a good deal more subtle. In a paper entitled "The Ordination of Women and the 'Maleness' of the Christ"[20] (published in 1976, written when he was a professor at the General Theological Seminary, in the run-up to the ECUSA General Convention debate on women in the priesthood), he develops an argument from the use of metaphor in classical Trinitarian theology.

The very title of Norris's piece is revealing in itself. The inverted commas speak volumes. Norris is clearly one who believes that sexual identity is largely, if not wholly, a social construct: that men and women are "the same thing with different fittings," and that "humanity" in some sense subsists apart from or beyond sexual differentiation. "The Christ," moreover, is a loaded term. It presupposes a clear divide between concept and person; between Jesus of Nazareth and "the Christ" of classical Christology. Norris wants to demonstrate that the Fathers shared the opinions of twentieth century liberal Christians about sex, and he does so by attacking, head-on, the idea that only a male can represent Christ at the altar as novel and dangerous. Like a clever undergraduate, he seeks cheekily to reverse received opinion: the present-day innovators prove to be the orthodox, and the conservatives the heretics. The notion that the Christian priesthood is male because it figures or represents a male savior, says Norris, is both modern and disturbing. "The argument is virtually unprecedented. It does not in fact

19. Cornwall, "Intersex & Ontology: A Response," 15.
20. Norris, "Ordination of Women and the 'Maleness,'" 71–85.

state any of the traditional grounds on which ordination to presbyterate or episcopate has been denied to women. To accept the argument and its practical consequence, therefore, is not to maintain tradition, but to alter it by altering its meaning." And he goes on to explain why. "The premises which apparently ground [the representative argument]," he claims, ". . . imply a false and dangerous understanding of the mystery of redemption—one which, if carried to its logical conclusion, would effectively deny the reality of Christ as the one in whom all things are 'summed up.'"

All this is itself novel and unfounded. There is, as Norris must have been aware, a long tradition which speaks of the priest and bishop as representing God, Father, and Son. Ignatius of Antioch refers to the bishop as "type of the Father";[21] the iconoclast controversy of the seventh and eighth centuries debated at length whether and how, in his particularity, the Incarnate Son should be depicted and represented;[22] and in the thirteenth century, Aquinas speaks of the priest as acting "in persona Christi."[23] There is, moreover, simply no evidence that Greek speakers of the third and fourth centuries shared Norris's concept of undifferentiated humanity, and much evidence (assiduously assembled by feminist scholars) to the contrary. The use of "anthropos" and "homo" in the languages of the societies in which they are rooted (patriarchies where women were in every sense unenfranchised) simply does not add up to the "inclusive humanity" which Norris and others want. With Plato and Aristotle, the Fathers regarded the subordination of women as "natural": women were unlike slaves in that they were free, but unlike men in that they were not politically active or competent. But there is more. What content, in any event, could the notion of "a Christ" possibly have, torn from its Judaic roots? The Christ the Fathers proclaimed is not merely a savior figure (Poseidon Soter, Zeus Soter, Dionysus Soter, Athena Soteira, Hecate Soteira, etc., etc.), but the sole fulfillment of messianic expectation: the Son of David. He is intelligible and identifiable only in terms of the cultural context from which he came and in which he lived. It is from that Jewish context that the maleness of Jesus derives its "soteriological significance."

The notion that women's ordination will in some way correct a current "imbalance" in religious imagery surfaces for the first time in the Episcopal Church in the United States. Bishop Paul Moore of New York,

21. St. Ignatius of Antioch, *Ad Trall*, 3,1:SCh 10,96; cf. *Ad Magn*, 6,1:SCh 10,82–84.

22. See Schoborn, *God's Human Face*, 133.

23. St. Thomas Aquinas, STh III,22,4c.

an early advocate of women's ordination in that Church, argued that the "maleness" of the deity might in some way be mitigated by the presence of female ministers.

> God as Father and God as Son invoked by a male minister during worship creates in the unconscious, the intuitive, the emotive part of your belief, an unmistakable male God. However, when women begin to read the Scripture, when they preside at the Eucharist, when they wear the symbolic robes of Christ, this unconscious perception will begin to be redressed and the femininity of God will begin to be felt.[24]

To this clumsy and confused thinking, Daphne Hampson provides us once more with a ready response.

> The difficulty . . . was brought home to me some years ago in attending a eucharistic liturgy, which I believe had been written by Carter Heyward . . . Only women were present and the service was orientated towards women. In place of a sermon there was a time of quiet in which women present spoke to the theme of "creation," some from the perspective of giving birth. How jarring it seemed then that, at the consecration, reference had necessarily to be made to the man Jesus of Nazareth: he had to take centre stage. Not simply was he mentioned, as men may well have been in the prayers of intercession, but he was actively made present as lord of the situation.[25]

She is again making a point which would not sound out of place in the mouths of traditionalist controversialists, Eric Mascall say, or V. A. Demant. Like Hampson, they would emphasise the anamnesis of Jesus, which lies at the heart of the catholic understanding of the eucharist. They would then go on to say, which might equally be thought to be implicit in Hampson's account of the Heyward "eucharist," that this necessary anamnesis is amplified and more fully expressed when the minister of the rite is himself a man.

* * *

Theology, it is sometimes said, is the only academic discipline in which primitive remains a term of approbation. So if the maleness of Jesus and its symbolic impact has proved to be problematic for Christian feminists, no

24. Moore, *Take a Bishop Like Me*, 37.
25. Hampson, *Theology and Feminism*, 62–63.

less so has been their relationship with the biblical and Christian past. Of course, feminist problems in relating to a patriarchalist past are not exclusive to Christians. In a ground-breaking book on women and drama in the age of Shakespeare, Lisa Jardine summarized two differing responses:

> There appear currently to be two main lines of approach to Shakespeare's drama within a feminist perspective . . . The first assumes that Shakespeare has earned his position at the heart of the traditional canon of English literature by creating characters who reflect every possible nuance of the richness and variety which is to be found in the world around us. His female characters in this view reflect accurately the whole range of specifically female qualities . . . The second line of approach assumes quite the opposite. Shakespeare's society is taken to be oppressively chauvinistic—a chauvinism whose trace is to be found in innumerable passing comments on women in the plays.[26]

For Shakespeare read Jesus—except that in the case of Jesus the two approaches have been melded into one, with a conspiracy theory to link them. Jesus was an egalitarian revolutionary, the theory goes, whose closest associates were so blinded by the ambient culture of misogyny that they could not grasp how radical he was. A male conspiracy, down the ages, has buried his insights under the dead weight of deepening patriarchy. Only in recent times has the truth about him come to light.

It is strange that Biblical scholars and Church historians have been slow to point out the near absurdity of all this. It is an axiom of social anthropology that in other cultures and former times, ethical assumptions which we make without question would have seemed outlandish and unintelligible. Imagine trying to explain the principles of the RSPCA to the clientele of the Colosseum. And yet the belief that a Palestinian rabbi of the first century (and later the greatest and most influential of his pharisaical converts) embraced a doctrine which was unknown before the eighteenth century Enlightenment and did not gain general credence until the 1920s has somehow passed virtually unquestioned.

Jesus, it is often said, was revolutionary in his attitude to women. Even the Roman Magisterium—eager no doubt to say something that might be construed as "positive"—has gone along with the notion.

> [Jesus's] attitude towards women was quite different from that of his milieu, and he deliberately and courageously broke with it. For

26. Jardine, *Still Harping on Daughters*, 1–2.

17

example, to the great astonishment of his own disciples Jesus con-
verses publicly with the Samaritan woman (cf. Jn 4:27); he takes no
notice of the state of legal impurity of the woman who had suffered
from haemorrhages (cf. Mt 9:20–22); he allows a sinful woman to
approach him in the house of Simon the Pharisee (cf. Lk 7:37ff.);
and by pardoning the woman taken in adultery, he means to show
that one must not be more severe towards the fault of a woman
than towards that of a man (cf. Jn 8:11). He does not hesitate to
depart from the Mosaic Law in order to affirm the equality of the
rights and duties of men and women with regard to the marriage
bond (cf. Mk 10:2–11; Mt 19:3–9).[27]

These claims are the subject of the next chapter. They prove, as we shall see, insubstantial if not totally unfounded. But take the story of Jesus and the Samaritan woman as an example. It is not a story about Jesus's attitude to women—indeed there are no stories in the Gospels "about" Jesus's attitude to women. It is not even a story "about" Jesus's relationship with a woman. It is hard to see what comfort a feminist might gain from it. The metaphorical association of Woman with marital and spiritual infidelity ("whoring after strange Gods" [cf. Hos 1:2]) looks suspiciously like misogyny, and the oblique references back to the meetings at wells of Isaac and Rebecca, Jacob and Rachel, have disturbing patriarchalist overtones. It is by no means certain, what is more, that the now famous ending to the tale (". . . they [the disciples] marveled that he was talking with a woman") can support the conclusion which has recently been drawn from it. The most natural inference, surely, is not that the disciples were amazed at what Jesus was in the habit of doing, but astounded that he had broken with the habits of a lifetime! If there is a lesson to be learned here it is about the difficulties inherent in seeking guidance from such texts on matters which they were never intended to address and which are strictly irrelevant to them. The fact that Christians have been dealing with texts in precisely that way for centuries is no excuse.

An older generation of feminists was right: for them the Bible is uncomfortable territory. Who, after all, could dispute the patriarchal credentials of the culture of the Old Testament, where male circumcision is the rite of entry into the community of Israel, where the cultic community was restricted to men, and where even sacrificial victims were required to be male (Lev 1:3)? And the same is largely true of the New Testament. "There is no positive evidence," says Hampson, "that Jesus saw anything wrong

27. Sacred Congregation, *Inter Insigniores*, para. 2.

with the sexism of his day."[28] And Nicola Slee provides some interesting statistics.[29] Of the main characters in Jesus's parables in Mark none are women; in Matthew there are eighty-five characters, of whom twelve are women (but ten are bridesmaids in one story!); in Luke there are 108, of whom nine are women. And this poor rating is capped, as traditionalists never tire in pointing out, by the appointment of the Twelve—patriarchs of the New Israel, and a missed opportunity if ever there was one.

For Christian feminists, what is more, Lisa Jardine's two conflicting approaches represent the clash of two contrasting cultures. Because Christianity is an historical religion in which "primitive" remains a term of approbation, more than nominal respect must be accorded the historical record. But sexual egalitarianism, as we have seen, is a recent development with its origins in the ideology of the Enlightenment. Church feminists, in consequence, find themselves co-belligerents with a class of persons whose posture toward the past might best be described as arrogance mingled with anger. "Men (sic) will never be free," wrote Denis Diderot, "until the last king is strangled with the entrails of the last priest."[30] They are not encouraging words for the priesting of women.

Much of the polemic against the Christian past marshalled by feminists has, in fact, been freely adapted from the writings of the radical Enlightenment. In Beverley Clack's exhaustive anthology *Misogyny in the Western Philosophical Tradition*,[31] Tertullian, Augustine, and Thomas Aquinas precede Descartes, Hobbes, Locke, Hume, Kant, and Rousseau. The irony is that much of the weaponry used against the former originated with the latter, and was part and parcel of their hatred of monasticism and contempt for celibacy. All this, it has to be said, is more prejudicial to their case than many Christian feminists have grasped. Christianity, as an historical religion, is essentially retrospective: it locates authority in past events. The Enlightenment project was essentially prospective: it looked to a progressively unfolding future. Anthony Pagden's characterization is apt:

> Unlike either the Renaissance or the Reformation, the Enlightenment had begun not as an attempt to rescue some hallowed past,

28. Hampson, *Theology and Feminism*, 88.

29. Slee, "Parables and Women's Experience," 25–31.

30. Attributed to Diderot by Jean-François de La Harpe in *Cours de Littérature Ancienne et Moderne*, 1840. A similar saying appears in Diderot's posthumous *Poesies Diverses*, 1875.

31. Clack, *Misogyny in the Western*.

but as an assault on the past in the name of the future. "If a century could be described as 'philosophical' merely because it rejected the wisdom of past centuries," wrote the mathematician and philosopher Jean D'Alembert ". . . then the eighteenth would have to be called the 'century of Philosophy par excellence.' It was a period which sought to overturn every intellectual assumption, every dogma, every "prejudice" (a favourite term) that had previously exercised any hold over the minds of men.[32]

Christian feminists need to be aware that association with those who entertain such contempt for the past (and the Christian past in particular) is worse than fraternizing with the enemy: it is tantamount to sawing off the branch on which they sit.

* * *

In feminist terms, the historical record is, as most secular feminists seem to agree, one of unbroken patriarchy and intermittent bouts of more or less serious misogyny. No age but the present is congenial to them. But there are those for whom such a bleak vision of the past is too much. If women and men are truly equal and in every respect socially equivalent things, they suppose, it must at some time have been more rosy. So the search was on. They persuaded themselves that in far flung places and at times far distant, things had been different: there must have been thriving matriarchal societies, which, alas fell in the course of time, to the rapacity of men. Primitive matriarchy, interestingly, was a speciality of Soviet and Chinese communist ideology. The Standard English language history of the People's Republic of China,[33] for example, begins with an account of matriarchal communities along the Yangtze valley around 2,500 BC. The claim is largely evidence-free (no explanation is offered of how such information could have been gleaned from the archaeological evidence). In less doctrinaire times it has been withdrawn. Christian feminists, as we shall see, have sought comfort in the speculative reconstruction of what have been called "the earliest Christianities," "fragments of a faith forgotten" located a lost Golden Age, among the papyri of the Egyptian desert and in the fragmented records of Gnostic communities long dead.

---

32. Pagden, *Enlightenment: Why it still Matters*, 26.
33. Shouyi and Yang, *Outline History of China*, 38.

More rationally, the question has to be why patriarchy endured so long and has been universal across cultures and continents. Is there, as some religious traditionalists have claimed, something "natural" or even inevitable about patriarchy? Is the scriptural imagery of a male God redeeming creation through the action of His Son grounded in a language written into the human genes and upon the human heart? Some modern theorists have concluded precisely that. Steven Goldberg's book of 1977, *The Inevitability of Patriarchy*,[34] with its exhaustive catalogue and systematic refutation of every recorded claim about the existence of matriarchal societies, was greeted with a predictable hail of criticism from left-leaning academe. More irritating to them still was a review of the first American edition, by the anthropologist Margaret Mead: "Persuasive . . . accurate. It is true, as Professor Goldberg points out that all the claims so glibly made about societies ruled by women are nonsense. We have no reason to believe that they ever existed . . . Men have always been the leaders in public affairs and the final authorities at home."[35]

Goldberg's thesis that social structures inevitably reflect and express essential biological, hormonal, and physical differences between women and men—despite its unpopularity in some quarters—has received a good deal of support in recent years from other analysts. The work of Simon Baron-Cohen[36] squarely confronts the received wisdom (current at least since John Stuart Mill's deeply flawed *The Subjection of Women*) that male and female are "social constructs." In a rather less theoretical mode, Steven Rhoads makes a case for adapting social policy to take account of the basic differences of aim and outlook between women and men.[37] He has shown, as one professor of anthropology tersely put it, that the "the Empress of androgyny has no clothes."[38]

Matriarchy, like the existence of Amazons, has always been located more in the imagination than in reality—in the territory of Rider Haggard, rather than that of serious anthropology. It is becoming increasingly clear that the notion of a feminist Jesus and a first century world peopled with Christian women priests is similarly inventive. These things never existed

---

34. Goldberg, *Inevitability of Patriarchy*.

35. Quoted on the dust jacket of the book in question, and by Goldberg himself in an article, "Feminism Against Science," in the *Journal of AIMHS*.

36. Baron-Cohen, *Essential Difference: Men, Women*.

37. Rhoads, *Taking Sex Differences Seriously*.

38. Publisher's blurb for Rhoads, *Taking Sex Differences Seriously*.

except in the minds of those who desperately want them to be so. They are myths answering a pressing need. That mythology is the subject of the chapters which follow. This is a book about the tales people tell when precedent is needed in order to justify an action for which there is no precedent.

* * *

We begin, necessarily, with Jesus. There has been, over the years, a recurrent, and perhaps understandable, attempt to harness the Son of God to every passing social and political bandwagon. C. S. Lewis identified this as the "Christianity and . . ." syndrome.

> My dear Wormwood,
>
> The real trouble about the set your patient is living in is that it is merely Christian. They all have individual interests, of course, but the bond remains mere Christianity. What we want, if men become Christians at all, is to keep them in the state of mind I call "Christianity And." You know—Christianity and the Crisis, Christianity and the New Psychology, Christianity and the New Order, Christianity and Faith Healing, Christianity and Psychical Research, Christianity and Vegetarianism, Christianity and Spelling Reform. If they must be Christians let them at least be Christians with a difference. Substitute for the faith itself some Fashion with a Christian colouring. Work on their horror of the Same Old Thing.[39]

"Study the New Testament," a Chartist newspaper, enjoined its readers in 1841, "it contains the elements of Chartism."[40] ". . . we are all priests," exclaims a character in Flaubert's *L'Education Sentimentale* (1869), "the workman is a priest like the founder of Socialism, the Master of us all, Jesus Christ!"[41] Since the almost routine nineteenth century identification of Christianity with soft-edged socialism the notion has come a long way. ("Christianity and vegetarianism" was Lewis's favorite.) The logic behind the syndrome is simple but fallacious: because Jesus was a Good Man he must necessarily have favored all that the protagonist thinks to be good. On grounds scarcely more sophisticated or informed, feminists have claimed him for their own. We need therefore to ask, "What did Jesus think about women?" And whether, in a modern analytical sense, he thought about women at all.

39. Lewis, *Screwtape Letters*, 97.

40. Norman, *Church and Society in England*, 262.

41. Flaubert, *Sentimental Education*, 303.

The chapter following deals with the claims repeatedly made about St. Paul. Feminists have always been in two minds about Paul. For a long time he was portrayed as an egregious example of the blanket misogyny of his era. Paul was said to be the crucial agent in the transformation of the counter-cultural, radically egalitarian "Jesus Movement" into an institutional church which oppressed women. The problem with this theory is the absence of any specific scriptural text establishing the alleged egalitarianism of Jesus. As we will see, Jesus never addresses the subject of the social or cultic status of women directly, and no firm conclusions can be drawn from his general conduct. This problem has been solved in a quite remarkable way. In a curious volte-face, Paul the hated misogynist was transformed into a feminist hero; and Galatians 3:28 has been drafted in to supply the pressing need for a biblical slogan. Of course, the *mulier tacet* texts (requiring women to stay silent), on which Paul's previous reprobation had been based, remained. They were now regarded, not as incontrovertible proofs of Paul's hatred of women, but either as later interpolations (by men who could not stomach the strong meat of Paul's radicalism), or as undesirable elements in Paul's own psycho-pathology (which the gospel values in him were struggling to suppress). Those who were in two minds about Paul had created an apostle in their own image; one who was in two minds about himself. The primary task of the exegete—to illuminate the text in its integrity in the light of its author's culture, background, and known mentality—was set aside, and the concerns of an age far removed from his own arbitrarily imposed upon it.

Chapter 4 is devoted to Mary of Magdala. For a character to whom there are only thirteen references in scripture (most of them cognate and only one outside the Paschal narratives), the Magdalen has had a long and eventful career. Since her death she has been credited with being, amongst other things, a prostitute, a penitent, an early migrant to the Côte d'Azur, the scion of a royal house, and, of course, the wife of God and mother of his grandson. For none of this is there a shred of firm evidence. That fact might have been read as a warning against further unwarranted speculation, but not so. Recent books about her range from the relatively scholarly to the frankly barking. She has emerged in Christian feminist polemic as "apostola Apostolorum" ("apostle to the Apostles"). The claim is based on the assertion that Mary was the first to see the risen Lord, and was charged by Him to proclaim the resurrection to others. As we shall see, there is no unequivocal support in scripture for either claim. Nor is it clear what effect, if any, the truth of the assertion would have on the restriction of episcopal office to men.

The next chapter is a round-up of some of the more specific (and imaginative) evidence which has been adduced for women priests in the early years of Christianity. The Roman Catacombs and the Colosseum have a special place in the popular mythology of early Christianity. Featured in Hollywood blockbusters and historical novels, the truth is that neither lives up to its reputation. There is no evidence that Christians were ever martyred in the Colosseum; nor were the catacombs used either as hiding places or as places of regular worship. But the mystique lingers on. Ever since the attention of non-specialists was drawn to it by Joan Morris,[42] a fresco in the Cappella Graeca in the so-called Catacomb of Priscilla has been a focus of misguided attention. Probably because of its resemblance to the most famous of all frescoes of the Last Supper (a group of figures at a table arranged to face the spectator), it has been claimed to be a representation of a concelebration of the Eucharist by women priests of the early second century. Or, according to another authority, Priscilla and Aquilla, that ubiquitous Pauline couple, celebrating the eucharist together with friends. All this is improbable in the highest degree. Representations of eucharistic celebrations are otherwise unknown in paleo-Christian art; concelebration is unheard of before the seventh century; and the fresco is dated by most authorities to the end of the third century, when Aquilla and his wife were long dead.

A mosaic in the chapel of S. Zeno in the titular church of Sta Prassede in Rome has been taken to be a portrait of a woman bishop, "Theodora Episcopa," the mother of Pope Paschal I. Though she has left no other testament to posterity, Theodora has been celebrated by members of the Movement for the Ordination of Women with an eponymous cocktail (sparkling wine and pomegranate juice, in the style of the more familiar Bellini and suitably purple). Meanwhile, a former editor of *The Catholic Herald* has eked out a slim volume, and a subsequent television documentary, by retelling the hoary legend of Pope Joan, in which surely even he could not bring himself to believe.

* * *

Christianity is an historical religion. It is related to a particular historical moment. The radical critique of Baruch Spinoza (and the post-Christian

42. Morris, J., *Against Nature and God.*

feminism of Daphne Hampson) bases itself on two principles: the absurdity of miracles and the need to treat scripture in the critical, analytical manner adopted with regard to all other texts since the age of humanism. The paradox is that Christianity is a religion compelled by its denial of Spinoza's first principle to the rigorous pursuit of his second. Its particular relationship to a moment in time requires of it the utmost rigor in apprehending that moment. To uncover "the Jesus of history" (as though there were some other Jesus who was in some way unhistorical) is, for Christians, to learn something of the mind of God. The Incarnation—the foundational miracle of the Faith—is precisely the place where event and revelation meet. The two are inseparable: he is both God and a man. God in Christ, as the fathers of the Seventh Council affirmed, can be (and must be) described or delineated—the verb they used was *perigraphein*. The Council wittily turned the tables on the vanquished iconoclasts: to claim that God is indescribable, they said, is to fall into the deadly danger of making Him in one's own image—the very idolatry of which the iconodules had been accused. And, one might add, the crime of which Albert Schweitzer thought the questers after the "historical Jesus" were guilty.

Whilst Islam is the religion of an inviolable text and a single language, the characteristic activity of Christians is translation. Jesus spoke Aramaic; the gospels and epistles were written in Greek; a Latin translation mediated the gospel message to Western Europe; vernacular translations (especially into English and German) were crucial in the development of early modern language and culture. The temptation has always been to mimic Islam and to canonise a particular text at a particular time. It has wisely been resisted. Translation is a delicate and subtle process. It demands different qualities and responses at different times. Consider the manifold difficulties of transposing Racine into modern English verse. Translation requires a deep historical insight and a lively imagination. These qualities have been tragically lacking among liberal Christians sympathetic to the feminist challenge. In place of historical sensitivity they have substituted cultural imperialism. They have recreated the Christian past in their own image. The flagship in this regard has been the campaign for so-called "inclusive language" in Bible translation and in the liturgy. Secular feminists, of course, have been busily policing the pronouns (with a degree of success) for at least three generations. Whether the abandonment of allegedly offensive terms like "actress" and "usherette" effected or reflected changes in general attitudes is obviously open to question. The campaign, however, had at least the merit of restricting itself to censorship of the present: there have not, so far as I know, been "inclusive language" versions of Homer or Virgil, Chaucer, Shakespeare, or Wordsworth. One can imagine the outrage in *academe* were such projects to be set in train. But there has been hardly a murmur from the academic community against the bowdlerisation of the Psalmist and the Evangelists by otherwise reputable Christian scholars, publishers, and institutions. The chapters which follow seek to show that this insensitivity to history is not restricted to language. It extends to include anachronistic and distorting conclusions in other areas. What the cult of "Inclusive language" has achieved in the realm of textual infidelity has, in these instances, simply been continued by other means.

2: What did Jesus Really Think about Women?

In Gospel research certainty is a very scarce commodity floating adrift in an ocean of probabilities.

—GEZA VERMES

Jesus was neither a misogynist nor a feminist; his interests simply lay elsewhere.

—JUDITH OCHSHORN

What did Jesus really think about women? The very question seems to invite anachronism. It seems to assume that Jesus thought about women in an analytical, politicized way. That, of course, is little short of absurd. Earlier ages and other cultures certainly debated the relations between women and men, and reached differing and conflicting conclusions. English readers will remember the extended debate on "sovereignty in marriage" in Chaucer's Canterbury Tales, and the Wife of Bath's combative contribution. But something new and determinative happened in the late seventeenth–early eighteenth century which changed the debate forever. The first stage of feminist consciousness, writes Gerda Lerner, is "the awareness of a wrong."[1] Judith Lorber takes the matter further: "the long term goal of feminism must be no less than the eradication of gender

1. Lerner, *Creation of Patriarchy*, 242.

as an organizing principle of post-industrial society."[2] This awareness of wrong, and the political analysis which follows from it, has its origins in the Enlightenment project. Writing in 1700, with an acute awareness of the constitutional implications of the Revolution of 1688, the Newcastle bluestocking Mary Astell was probably the first to argue that if absolute rule is illegitimate in the state, it ought also to be so in the family. She is wittily reversing the arguments of Sir Robert Filmer's *Patriarcha*, the textbook of Stuart absolutism.

> Again, if absolute Sovereignty be not necessary in a State how comes it to be so in a Family? Or if so in a Family why not in a State, since no Reason can be alleged for the one that will not hold more strongly for the other? If Authority of the Husband, so far as it extends, is sacred and inalienable, why not that of the Prince? The Domestic Sovereign is without Dispute elected; and the Stipulations and Contract are mutual; is it not then partial in Men to the last Degree to contend for and practice that Arbitrary Dominion in their Families which they abhor and exclaim against in the State?[3]

Mary Astell's sagacity and wit, summoning the revolution in English politics to the aid of her feminist agenda, is remarkable; but that is not the end of the story. We know that Astell had read Hobbes and Locke (the weakness of whose argument for domestic authority she here deftly exposes). Spinoza was to her probably no more than the name of a bogeyman. But the role of Spinoza's metaphysics in the revolution in European consciousness—even, perhaps especially, among those who were eager to dissociate themselves from him—is undeniable. A contemporary of Astell who knew the work both of Pierre Bayle and Benedict de Spinoza was Bernard Mandeville, whose first prose work in English, *The Virgin Unmask'd* (1709),[4] must have been music to Astell's ears. Mandeville is fulsome about the utter defenselessness under the law of women trapped by marriage to cruel, selfish, and domineering husbands. He attacked at the same time both the rigidity of the English divorce laws and the doctrine of the indissolubility of marriage. He was convinced of "the parity of the intellectual organs in both sexes, and that woman's wit is equal to man's." Mandeville, a native of Dort, settled in England in the aftermath of the Glorious Revolution, bring-

2. Lorber, "Dismantling Noah's Ark," 58.
3. Astell, "Some Reflections on Marriage," 563.
4. Mandeville, *Virgin Unmask'd*.

ing with him egalitarian notions learnt in Holland, to unite with the native Hobbesian radicalism.

It was, however, a revolution more fundamental and more radical than that of 1688 that brought the feminism of the early Enlightenment to its apogee. *The Declaration of the Rights of Woman* was Olympe de Gouges's response to the exclusion of women from the French National Constituent Assembly's *Declaration of the Rights of Man and of the Citizen (August 26, 1789)*. It earned Olympe, a butcher's daughter and playwright, her day at the guillotine.

> Consequently, the sex that is as superior in beauty as it is in courage during the sufferings of maternity recognizes and declares in the presence and under the auspices of the Supreme Being, the following Rights of Woman and of Female Citizens:
>
> *Article I*: Woman is born free and lives equal to man in her rights. Social distinct can he based only on the common utility.
>
> *Article II*: The purpose of any political association is the conservation of the natural and imprescriptible rights of woman and man; these rights are liberty, property, security, and especially resistance to oppression.
>
> *Article III*: The principle of all sovereignty rests essentially with the nation, which a nothing but the union of woman and man; no body and no individual can exercise any authority which does not come expressly from it (the nation).
>
> *Article IV*: Liberty and justice consist of restoring all that belongs to others, thus, the only limits on the exercise of the natural rights of woman are perpetual male tyranny, these limits are to be reformed by the laws of nature and reason.
>
> *Article V*: Laws of nature and reason proscribe all acts harmful to society; everything which is not prohibited by these wise and divine laws cannot be prevented, and no one can be constrained to do what they do not command.
>
> *Article VI*: The law must be the expression of the general will; all female and male citizens must contribute either personally or through their representatives to its formation, it must be the same for all: male and female citizens, being equal in the eyes of the law, must be equally admitted to all honours, positions and public

employment according to their capacity, and without other distinctions besides those of their virtues and talents.[5]

And so on, through another sixteen articles. What is clear, in article after
article, is de Gouge's almost casual identification of divine with natural
law—*Deus sive natura*. Hers is a largely unconscious association of demo-
cratic politics, *a priori* egalitarianism, an abhorrence of hierarchies, and the
new metaphysics of the radical Enlightenment. It is a heady combination,
which, as one might expect, Daphne Hampson, in our own day, eagerly
embraces.

> One may believe of God that God is equally available to people
> in all times and places. Such is my position. That is to say I deny
> that there could be a particular revelation of God in any one age
> which henceforth becomes normative for all others . . . I am not a
> Christian because I do not credit, as I earlier put it, that nature and
> history could be other than closed causal nexuses or believe that
> there can be events which are in some way qualitatively different
> from other events.[6]

She goes on to point out that this *a priori* position has a compelling ethical
dimension.

> The question of the truth of the Christian picture of the world has
> increasingly come to be raised during the last two hundred years.
> In our age this has become an urgent question for many people
> and many others have left Christianity behind. The further ques-
> tion which feminism raises—to an extent which, I would contend,
> this has not been raised before—is that of whether it is moral . . .
> [or] . . . false to one's belief in human equality.[7]

Anyone following the trajectory of feminism from Mary Astell to Daphne
Hampson will be acutely aware that it begins a thousand miles from the
world view of first century Jewry and moves inexorably away from it. Upon
no presently agreed historical principle could Jesus be thought to have any
place on that trajectory or even any inkling of the principles which governed it.

So, if Jesus was not—could not have been—a feminist, what *did* he
think about women? How can we know? And does it matter anyway? It is

5. Gouges, "Declaration of the Rights of Woman," 612–13.

6. Hampson, *Theology and Feminism*, 41.

7. Ibid., 45.

a remarkable fact that traditionalists and feminists have found a degree of agreement on the subject. Both have supposed that he was at variance with the culture of his time. Their agreement involves divergent but related views of the significance of Jesus's choice of twelve male apostles. Traditionalists see the choice of an all-male apostolate as crucially significant for future developments. It was an exceptional event, contrary they say to Jesus's habitual attitude to women. As such it was determinative; it determined the constitution of the Apostolic Ministry for all time.

> Wherefore, in order that all doubt may be removed regarding a matter of great importance, a matter which pertains to the Church's divine constitution itself, in virtue of my ministry of confirming the brethren (cf. Lk 22:32) I declare that the Church has no authority whatsoever [declaramus Ecclesiam facultatem nullatenus habere] to confer priestly ordination on women and that this judgment is to be definitively held by all the Church's faithful.[8]

> Pope John Paul II has made it clear that his office is to restate authoritatively and clearly the tradition of the Church: that Our Lord Chose only male apostles, and that his example is binding on the Church for all time . . . There is therefore almost a presumption in this report—a presumption that we may indeed *justify the ways of God to man*.[9]

Feminists, on the other hand, think that Jesus's supposed habitual inclusion and encouragement of women simply demonstrates that his choice in the matter of Apostles was not his own. He was conditioned by the ambient culture. Jesus wanted to appoint female apostles; but knew in pragmatic terms that they would be unacceptable to those among whom they must work. His choice, in consequence, has little or no significance for the future.

Notice that both sides are agreed that Jesus envisaged a future in which his choice in the matter of apostles would be significant (or not!). But what if he had no future in mind? Of course it will be necessary to examine in detail every recorded encounter of Jesus with women in order to assess the credibility of the claims made about them. But it will be as well to begin by explaining that the cross-party consensus—that Jesus differed in his attitudes to women from those around him, and that his choice of male apostles had enduring significance—challenges some recent trends in the Quest for the Historical Jesus.

8. John Paul II, "Ordinatio Sacerdotalis," para. 4.

9. Baker, *Consecrated Women*, 6–7.

There are two kinds of truth about Jesus. The first is the truth attested by faith and found in the Gospels and later in the formularies of the Church. It involves, amongst other things, a wholesale acceptance of the place of Jesus in a salvation history extending through the Old Testament and beyond. The second kind of truth can claim less certainty than faith; it hangs on "scientific" historical inquiry. The second kind can claim no finality; historical research can never retrieve more than a part of the truth. It may even prove to be a very small part. The first kind of truth deals in metaphors, assertions, and affirmations; the second in guesses, surmises, and speculations. The Jesus Seminar, for example, which has made a significant contribution to the Quest for the Historical Jesus, even puts its conclusions to the vote. An important part of the search for an historically credible Jesus is the development of a technique for determining which of the sayings in the Gospels are his own words and which are the embellishments of the gospel writers, in the service of their own distinctive theologies. Two conflicting techniques have recently held the field. We will call them techniques of dissimilarity and similarity.

Similarity first. In the 1970s, fuelled by some remarkable archaeological discoveries, the Quest shifted gear. The early twentieth century emphasis had been on form criticism and the Hellenistic background of the early Church. Now the Jewish context came to play an increasing part, as the titles of more recent books show: *Jesus the Jew* (1973); *Jesus and Judaism* (1985); *The Historical Jesus: The Life of a Mediterranean Jewish Peasant* (1991); *A Marginal Jew: Rethinking the Historical Jesus* (1991–2001); and *Jesus of Nazareth, King of the Jews: A Jewish Life and the Emergence of Christianity* (1999). With help from the Dead Sea Scrolls, the voluminous works of Flavius Joseph, and new insights into early rabbinic literature, Questers were beginning to identify the "authentic" sayings of Jesus as those which blended well into his Jewish background and could easily be distinguished from the Hellenistic overtones of the evangelists, who were Greek speakers, writing for a largely Gentile audience.

At the same time other scholars, mostly in the United States, were taking an opposite tack. Dissimilarity was the watchword of the Jesus Seminar. They placed an equal and opposite emphasis on the separation of Jesus from his cultural context. The Seminar put considerable emphasis on irony and the adversative character of Jesus's preaching: a characteristic of his style, they thought, was the desire to outrage or to reverse expectations: "Love your enemies." In consequence, they assumed that if a saying was rooted in traditional Judaism, without that controversialist element of surprise, it was unlikely to be his. Naturally, this assumption had its critics. It excised Jesus from his environment, it was said, in a way which would surely have made it the harder for him to have influence on it. It posited an eccentric Jesus, said others, "who learned nothing from his own culture and made no impact on his followers."

Then there is the matter of eschatology. Largely under the influence of Albert Schweitzer and Johannes Weiss, the majority of Questers in the early part of the twentieth century accepted the idea that the Jesus Movement was an apocalyptic movement, expecting the Kingdom of God (however that was envisaged) to arrive by some dramatic intervention during the ministry of Jesus. This was, of course, an acute embarrassment to Christians, for if it were true then Jesus had been misguided. The English scholar C. H. Dodd developed an ingenious theory of "realized eschatology": Jesus, he claimed, thought that the kingdom was in some sense in the future and yet that, in some sense, it had already come in his own words and deeds. The notion did not fly for very long. More recently the Seminar has concluded that Jesus did not expect a future kingdom in any sense at all. His message was about the here and now, and he did not expect any dramatic intervention by God. Instead his ministry was one of political, social, and economic reform. The Jesus Seminar has, of course, been accused (as Schweitzer had accused earlier Questers) of creating a Jesus in its own image. Certainly, following on from its characterization of him as a master of paradox, a sort of peasant Oscar Wilde, the idea that he was a social reformer with no practical agenda for the implementation of his program stretches the imagination somewhat.

All this—you will be way ahead of me by now—feeds directly into the debate about Jesus's attitude to women. If similarity is seen as the governing criterion of authenticity (the majority view), then both sides in the argument over women's ordination have got it wrong. If dissimilarity rules, then both gain some credibility. The decisive factor, in that event, becomes eschatology, where neither party comes off very well. Both assume that, in one way or another, Jesus intended a Church and had a message for it. None of the current Questers, it need hardly be said, supposes that remotely to be the case.

It will be as well then to list all Jesus's encounters with women, and deal with them each in turn: Peter's mother-in-law (Matt 8:14–15), (Mark 1:30–31), (Luke 4:38–39); the woman who touched Jesus' garment (Mark

5:25–34); the daughter of Jairus (Mark 5:35–43); the widow of Nain (Luke 7:11–17); the woman bent double (Luke 13:10–17); a poor widow's offering (Luke 21:1–4); the woman taken in adultery (John 7:53–8:11); the woman at the well in Samaria (John 4:1–42); the Syrophoenician woman (Mark 7:24–30), (Matt 15:21–28); Martha and Mary (Luke 10:38–42), (John 11:1–44); the anointing in Bethany (John 12:1–8); the anointing by a repentant sinner (Luke 7:36–50).

* * *

It is quite a list. New Testament scholar Frank Stagg and classicist Evelyn Stagg[10] have claimed that the synoptic Gospels contain a relatively high number of references to women. Evangelical Bible scholar Gilbert Bilezikian agrees,[11] especially by comparison with literary works from the same period. These claims are based on their own expertise and experience and are obviously difficult for the general reader to verify. But what is indisputable is that the references are numerous. We need to know whether this frequency is exceptional for a Jew of the period, and what is the significance, individually and collectively, of the incidents themselves.

In the hectic opening section of Mark's Gospel, the healing of *Peter's mother-in-law* has an important place. The passage is similarly positioned by Matthew and Luke; it does not occur in John. After the exorcism of a demoniac in the Capernaum synagogue, Jesus enters the house of Simon, whom he has just encountered by the lakeside and called to discipleship. This domestic environment—Jesus is elsewhere said to be "at home" in Capernaum—is the setting for a healing which confirms the new relationship with Peter. The mother-in-law is taken by the hand (Matthew and Mark) or the fever is rebuked (Luke) and she "serves" them. It has been suggested (perhaps influence by the AV translation "ministered to them") that the verb here has a wider than domestic connotation. The context makes this highly unlikely. Peter's mother-in-law serves those who have recently come under her roof and so require her hospitality: Jesus, James, and John.

The healing of *the woman who touched Jesus's garment* raises issues about Jesus's relation to the provisions of the Torah. The woman's condition disqualified her from marriage (Lev 20:18) as well as religious life in general (Lev 15:25–33). She ritually contaminated those with whom she came

10. Stagg and Stagg, *Woman in the World of Jesus.*
11. Bilezikian, "Renouncing the Love of Power," 53.

into contact. In societies where women are fulfilled, legitimated, given full membership of the community, and cared for in old age by their children, hers was a tragedy which ostracized and isolated her. Jesus gives her back not only her health, but also her dignity and her place in society. It is worth noting that the woman with an issue of blood, like some other New Testament characters, has developed a legend of her own. No less an authority than Eusebius recounts a visit he himself made to the woman's hometown.

> ... there stands upon an elevated stone, by the gates of her house, a brazen image of a woman kneeling, with her hands stretched out, as if she were praying. Opposite this is another upright image of a man, made of the same material, clothed decently in a double cloak, and extending his hand toward the woman. At his feet, beside the statue itself, is a certain strange plant, which climbs up to the hem of the brazen cloak, and is a remedy for all kinds of diseases. They say that this statue is an image of Jesus. It has remained to our day, so that we ourselves also saw it when we were staying in the city.[12]

Presumably with blood as the common factor, the woman was also later conflated with Veronica ("true image"), herself, of course, a pious fiction. We see here, in little, the same efflorescence of legend that reaches its culmination in the stories surrounding Mary Magdalen.

The raising of *Jairus's daughter* is an unusual "wrap-around" to the previous story. As often in Jesus's miracles, the role of family is crucial. Along with his own inner circle (Peter, James, and John) he takes the parents of the girl into the room where she is laid out. He takes her hand and speaks to her in Aramaic. Is this a vivid touch by Mark, or is the phrase "talitha cum," as Sanders speculates, tantamount to a spell or incantation?

Family is important in a rather different way in the story of *the widow of Nain*. In a patriarchal society in which the worth and dignity of women is defined in terms of their relationship with men, the death of the only son of a widow is both a financial and a social disaster. Jesus returns the son to his mother, and in doing so restores her place in the community. Widows feature largely in the Old Testament. Care for widows and orphans was deemed a particular religious duty (Deut 14:29, 24:17, etc.). Readers of the gospels would have been familiar with the story of Elijah and the widow of Zarephath.

---

12. Eusebius Pamphilius, *Ecclesiastical History*, cap. 18, paras. 1–3.

The story of *the woman bent double* is part of a group of stories about Sabbath healings and the resultant controversy. It is also an exorcism story. The woman is "untied" from her affliction as animals are untied in order to be led to food and water. A similar argument (this time involving a sheep fallen into a pit) is to be found at Matthew 12:7. The phrase "daughter of Abraham" occurs nowhere else in the New Testament. It has been suggested that this indicates a respect for women as full members of the covenant community, which is thought to be peculiar to Jesus. The title "son of Abraham" is likewise used only once, also by Luke (Luke 19:9).

Of the story of *the poor widow's offering* (the widow's mite), it is enough to point out that it is again a story about a widow.

The story of *the woman taken in adultery* appears not to have found a secure place in the New Testament until a relatively late date and was probably unknown to some of the early church fathers. The earliest manuscripts of John do not contain it, and it later found a place not only after John 7:52, but in one manuscript after John 7:36 and in some others after John 21:24. Other manuscripts insert it also after Luke 21:38. The translators of the Jerusalem Bible are alone, I think, in claiming that the episode is in "the style of the Synoptics." The structure of the tale—with its formulaic repetition of "writing on the ground" and the silent withdrawal of the accusers "one by one beginning with the eldest"—has a literary ring to it which, whilst not alien in tone to John's Gospel, raises questions as to its historicity. The moral—that repentance often begins from affirmation rather than condemnation—is in tune with much of Jesus's teaching.

The story of Jesus and *the woman at the well in Samaria* also raises questions of historicity. There is, of course, nothing impossible or intrinsically incredible about the tale. But its obvious symbolic structure and gnomic language are issues in themselves. It will be as well to list other reasons for supposing that the passage might be an editorial construct.

I. The story (whose possible sources are, for the most part, either Jesus or the woman herself) fits all too neatly into the image patterns of the Gospel (Jesus is real food; Jesus is real drink; etc.).

II. It involves an explicit claim by Jesus to divinity, in the *ego eimi* form familiar elsewhere in John.

III. The story ends with the conversion of numbers of Samaritans, on the testimony of the woman, and the conversion of other Samaritans as a result of the preaching of Jesus. This clearly anticipates the Gentile mission of the early church and the mission of Philip (Acts 8:4ff.), but it reads oddly alongside the Synoptic tradition and the specific charge to the Twelve at Matt 10:5–6 ("Do not go into the way of the Gentiles, and do not enter any city of the Samarians, but go rather to the lost sheep of the house of Israel").

IV. In common with other episodes in John's Gospel (including the woman taken in adultery) this passage has a developed literary style which makes it extremely difficult to disentangle editorial additions from traditional material.

It has been claimed that various aspects of the story illuminate Jesus's attitude to women. For example, that he speaks to a woman alone and without other male or female company, despite the provisions of the Mishnah.

> A man may not remain alone with two women, but a woman may remain alone with two men. Rabbi Simeon says: Even one man may remain alone with two women when his wife is with him, and he may sleep with them in an inn, because his wife watches over him.[13]

It is said that he is talking theology with a woman, despite an alleged taboo.

But both these observations fail to give weight to the symbolic nature of the exchange. The important thing is that the woman is a *Samaritan*. She needs to be a *woman* because she is representing the apostasy of the *Samaritans* (religious apostasy is conventionally represented in the Old Testament by marital infidelity, of which she turns out to be a startling example). The Samaritans were accused by orthodox Jews of syncretism, as evinced by Josephus (Ant 12.5.5). Note that neither Jesus nor the Evangelist seems to have any embarrassment about this traditional characterization of infidelity as a female trait. Jesus talks (rather gnomic) theology with her because this is not a story about his relations with a woman (or with womankind) but about the relation of the Messiah to the salvation of non-Jews. (John 4:22 "salvation is from the Jews"). The disciples are surprised to find Jesus talking alone with a woman (not, the narrator is implying, something they have previously encountered). They seek no explanation. It is hard to imagine, in the circumstances, what explanation might have been forthcoming.

The Syrophoenician woman (also described as a "Greek") approaches Jesus when, presumably because Pharisaic antagonism is intensifying, he is in hiding among non-Jews. The exchange here contrasts with the oblique

---

13. Danby, *The Mishnah*, Kid 4:12.

Johannine dialogue of double meanings between Jesus and the woman at the well. It has been suggested that Jesus is bested in repartee by the Syrophoenician, and that it is out of amused admiration that he grants her request. That, one suspects, is not how a contemporary Jew would have assessed the situation. They would have seen that only when the woman willingly conceded the lower status of foreigners ("dogs" not "children") did Jesus perform the healing, which he had at first refused. It was "because of this word" that Jesus acted; a word not clever but, in the context of the rabbinic teaching of his time, true.

Both Luke and the Fourth Gospel record a relationship with *Martha and Mary*. In John it has the added intimacy which results from Jesus's friendship with Lazarus and the miracle of his resuscitation. According to John (but not Luke) the relationship with the sisters was secondary to Jesus's friendship with their brother. Much has been made of the short account in Luke of Jesus's visit to the sisters' house. Some have waxed lyrical:

> Luke's story of Jesus in the home of Martha and Mary puts him solidly on the side of the recognition of the full personhood of woman with the right to options for her own life. In socializing with both sisters and in defending Mary's right to a role then commonly denied a Jewish woman, Jesus was following his far-reaching principle of human liberation.[14]

We have a right to ask what, shorn of the jargon of the late twentieth century, this really means. And to wonder how it relates to the text in question. The argument seems to turn on the assumption that Jesus (as a "Rabbi"—which he was in no formal sense) was breaking with custom and tradition by teaching a woman in her own home; and that Mary, in listening attentively to an interesting visitor, was making what is now called a "lifestyle choice." Neither assumption is sustainable. The Rabbis made a clear distinction between public instruction (the participation of women in the religious life of the community) and instruction at home—as, of course, does Paul at 1 Corinthians 14:35. Jesus, then, is doing nothing remarkable or exceptional. There is, moreover, no reason at all to suppose that Mary's disposition on this particular evening led to anything approaching a life-long commitment. Uncongenial as it might be to the modern mind, this passage has traditionally been deployed to point the distinction between the active and contemplative life in religious communities of women. That, too, is a homiletic trope which gains little encouragement from the actual

14. Stagg and Stagg, *Woman in the World of Jesus*, 119.

text. One simply cannot deduce sweeping and enduring principles from evidence so slight and circumstantial.

By contrast with Luke, John's story of the raising of Lazarus has Martha, not Mary, as its main protagonist. It is she who makes the initial profession of faith (later to be echoed by Mary). The details of this story must be read in relation to John's account of the resurrection of Jesus—a connection which is made explicit by the anointing in chapter twelve, reference to which is made here (John 11:2). The length of time in the grave, the positioning of the grave clothes (both the head-cloth and the rest) and the smell all relate to the events of Easter morning. This is the heart of the matter, and the primary function of the narrative. It is hard to see how any conclusion about Jesus's attitude to women can confidently be drawn from the roles of Martha and Mary in this relation of events. It is not a story about them. Some have suggested that the "many Jews" who came to believe in Jesus as a result of this miracle did so, at least in part, as a result of their association with Mary, whom they had come to visit and console. If so, she clearly had an equal and opposite affect on those other Jews who went off to incite hatred of him among the Pharisees and chief priests.

The *anointing at Bethany*, apart from minor details—the naming of the woman and the placing of the ointment—seems to be the same story we also encounter at Mark 14:2–9 and Matt 26:6–13 (which are almost identical with each other). This raises the problem of how all three relate to the story of "the woman who had a bad name in the town" at Luke 7:36–50. Much ink has been expended on this thorny topic. On September 21, 591, however, during a sermon delivered in the basilica of San Clemente in Rome, Pope Gregory the Great solved the conundrum (of which, in its modern form, he was, of course, unaware). He simply collapsed into one four distinct women: Luke's sinner; the woman in the house of Simon the Leper (Mark and Matthew); Mary of Bethany, the sister of Martha (Luke and John); and Mary of Magdala. He had, at a single stroke, created a figure with a lurid past, a compelling psychological history, pious siblings, and a starring role in the most momentous event in human history. His creation was an almost instant success; though even her most ardent devotees in the Middle Ages cannot have envisaged her subsequent career on the London stage. That woman is the subject of chapter three of this book. She acts here as a reminder of the dangers of alienating elements of the gospel record from their immediate context in the narrative, and from their place in the evangelists' work as a whole. The Bethany anointings in Matthew,

Mark, and John are all preparations for, and in a sense anticipations of, the Passion. The anonymous woman in the synoptics and Mary the sister of Martha are drawn proleptically into that drama. They are fulfilling—like the other women in the Passion narratives—time-honored female roles as the ones who keen over the deceased and who prepare the body for burial.

The *anointing by a repentant sinner* in Luke's Gospel has a quite different context and meaning. Like the story of the woman taken in adultery, it is about forgiveness. There is perhaps a deliberate ambiguity in the grammar of Luke 7:47—was the woman forgiven because she loved so much; or conversely did she love so much because she knew herself to be forgiven? The parable of the two debtors, which interrupts the action, suggests the latter. A sub-plot in the story is the tension between Simon and Jesus. Simon thinks that Jesus's failure to discern the woman's status and reputation casts doubt on his claim to be a prophet. Jesus proves his credentials by discerning Simon's inmost thoughts.

* * *

It will be evident from this brief survey that no consistent theme or pattern emerges from these various encounters with women. Jesus is compassionate, understanding, and perceptive. He treats with generosity and sympathy the predicaments of the women he encounters. What is absent—from these stories at least—is any anger at society's mistreatment of women in general. The hemorrhaging woman, to modern eyes, is the victim of cruel discrimination. Jesus heals her and commends her faith: there is no hint, however, of a will or intention to change the religious taboos which have added to her suffering. Nor is there evidence, as is sometimes claimed, that in his relationship with Mary of Bethany Jesus is deliberately challenging social attitudes. Nothing in their friendship, from the limited information we have, transgresses Rabbinical propriety. The meeting with the Samaritan woman at Jacob's well, if we feel able to disentangle an actual event from the evangelist's theologizing, would seem to be the only account of Jesus alone with a woman until after the resurrection. But John is careful to tell us of the disciples' astonishment at the fact. From that we can be assured that it was a singular occurrence.

Nor is the subject matter of Jesus's discourse or the language in which it is couched of much comfort to those searching for feminist sympathies. It has already been noted that the characters in Jesus's parables are predominantly male (193 males to 21 females). Women, it has been observed, are generally portrayed in them as fulfilling stereotypically female roles. But things are worse than that. Even the one who sews patches on garments and who knows not to sew unshrunk cloth on an old garment is masculine at Mark 2:21. In Mark's miraculous feeding there are five thousand men. Matthew is something less than gracious when he adds, "not to mention women and children." It is presumably this relentlessly androcentric language which modern "inclusive" translations exist to obscure.

Two other pieces of evidence need to be examined, however, before general conclusions can be reached.

Luke includes in his account of Jesus's ministry in Galilee information about a group of women that accompanied Jesus and the Twelve and "ministered" to them "out of their possessions." Mark (and Matthew following him) confirms the same information in their narratives of the Passion (Mark 15:40; Matt 27:55; Luke 23:49). Luke gives us a few names from the "many": Mary Magdalene, Joanna the wife of Chuza, Herod's steward, and Susanna. Matthew extends this list: Mary the mother of James and Joseph and the mother of Zebedee's sons. Mark adds Salome. Speculation as to the role and identity of these women has been rife. The verb "ministered" (Luke's word has the same root as deacon) has led to suggestions that the women shared in some way the evangelistic tasks of the Twelve— though the proviso "out of their possessions" suggests a somewhat more domestic function—the practical provision of food, clothing, and shelter. It has been suggested that they were women of "private means," and so perhaps with an interesting past (Mary of Magdala) or influential connections (Joanna, wife of Chuza). But it is best to stick to what we certainly know. Some had been healed, says Luke, from demons and infirmities: the Magdalen, in particular, had been exorcised of seven devils. But Luke has not given us the full story. Some of the women may indeed have had cures at the hands of Jesus and be following him out of gratitude and admiration. But others in the group had quite different reasons for their ministry: the mothers of James and Joseph, and of Zebedee's boys were sustaining and supporting family members. They were (perhaps understandably) concerned that the Son of Man had nowhere to lay his head and feared that their progeny might share the same experience. How many of the "many" fitted into which category we simply cannot say.

Mary of Magdala, of course, has long been the subject of extravagant speculation. More recently Joanna, Chuza's wife has been the object of exhaustive erudition by Professor Richard Bauckham of the University of St. Andrews.[15] He adduces evidence which traces Joanna from the single mention in Luke's Gospel to an apostolic career in Rome as the Junia who makes a fleeting appearance, along with an Andronicus, at the conclusion of the letter to the Romans. There can be no more poignant testimony to the paucity of evidence of female involvement in the mission and ministry of Jesus (and to the insatiable appetite for more of it) than to dedicate one hundred and fifteen pages of arduous scholarship to two passing references—scarcely thirty words in the Greek New Testament (see below: Alas, Poor Andronicus!).

The second piece of evidence is Jesus's choice of twelve male apostles. Why were all twelve men? Evelyn and Frank Stagg put the question forcibly:

> This is the strongest single evidence against a clear breakthrough on the part of Jesus in the recognition of the full equality of women with men. Apostleship was a role of distinction and a primary one in the early church. Why men only? The New Testament gives no clear answer . . . even in the example of Jesus there is not a complete overcoming of male bias.[16]

Their prime concern is the ordination of women; so, naturally, they view the matter almost exclusively in that light. They take it for granted that Jesus was an inclusive sort of fellow, like themselves. When he fails to show clear signs of being so, they pay him the compliment of supposing that he was nevertheless striving to "overcome male bias."

Both sides in the women priests debate routinely assume that the choice of the Twelve relates in some way to subsequent Christian ministry. But the issue of women's ordination is surely a distraction. The question of why Jesus chose twelve male apostles cannot be answered solely in terms of an outcome of which his original audience (including the Twelve themselves) were necessarily ignorant. Signs are generally addressed to an audience likely understand them. We need, in consequence, to be looking for a meaning or significance readily intelligible among early first century Jews. And it is not far to seek. Jesus, we can be reasonably sure, expected, in his own lifetime or very soon thereafter, a cosmic event which would inaugurate the reign and kingdom of God. We can be sure that this was central to his teaching for the simple reason that, though it had failed to materialize by the time the gospels were written (and though Paul had earlier felt it

15. Bauckham, *Gospel Women*, 109–99.

16. Stagg and Stagg, *Woman in the World of Jesus*, 123.

necessary to dampen the apocalyptic ardour of his Thessalonians), it still has a prominent place in the Synoptic tradition. This imminent in-breaking of the Kingdom, moreover, was clearly the expectation of the disciples. James and John sought positions of influence in the coming Kingdom, and Jesus himself promised that the Twelve would sit on thrones judging the twelve tribes. Part of this lively expectation was the conviction that the old pre-exilic Israel of twelve (rather than two) tribes would, in some miraculous way, be reconstructed by God. The whole nation, mythically founded on the offspring of the twelve sons of Jacob, would be brought together once more under divine rule. It is significant that, though there is no strong and unvarying tradition as to the names of the twelve, the number twelve was important enough to require the speedy election of Matthias. And the earliest witness to it is to be found in the earliest list of resurrection appearances (1 Cor 15:3–8). For the sign of Twelve to be intelligible, they of course had to resemble what they signified. Any twelve would not do: they had to be male Jews. This college of the Twelve, rooted in Jewish expectation, continued to be significant for the eschatology of the earliest Christians, even when others—Paul and James for example—had assumed positions in the community arguably more important than some of them.

This notion that the maleness and Jewishness of the Twelve—both bones of contention among feminists and their supporters—were necessary to its very function as a proleptic symbol of the coming kingdom does not, of course, necessarily rule out the possibility that Jesus had other ends in mind. It does not rule out that he intended what others, at that time, could not know: a church with Peter at its head and the twelve apostles as the foundation stones of its order and authority. That would be "reconstitution" of a related but more radical kind. What it does rule out is the idea that the choice of twelve men was somehow forced upon Jesus by the pragmatic requirements of his mission. The Twelve men were integral to the Mission. In choosing twelve males to figure the reconstituted twelve tribes, descended from the twelve sons of Israel, Jesus was consciously employing—and reinforcing—the patriarchal language of a world-view very far from that of modern feminism.

What E. P. Sanders has called "restoration eschatology"[17] also helps unravel the confusion about Jesus and divorce. The prohibition of divorce appears a total of four times in the synoptics and once in Paul: Matt 5:31ff., 19:3–9; Mark 10:2–12; Luke 16:18; 1 Cor 7:10f. There is a long form of the

17. Sander, *Historical Figure of Jesus*, 186.

saying (Mark 10:2–12 and Matt 19:3–9) and a short form (Matt 5:31f. and Luke 16:18). Paul is closer to the short form. This makes the prohibition of divorce the best attested of all Jesus's sayings. There can be little doubt, then, that Jesus was against divorce and forbade remarriage. Paul, scrupulous as ever, distinguishes his own opinion from the dominical dictum, allowing his readers to make their own assessment of a situation (marriage of a Christian to a non-believer) on which, in the nature of the case, there could be no "word from the Lord."

Jesus explains the prohibition (which ends a permissive provision of the Torah) by a joint appeal to the two creation narratives of Genesis: from the beginning God "made them male and female" (Gen 1:17), which is why a man must leave his father and mother "and the two become one body" (Gen 2:24). Jesus is appealing from the pragmatic ("because you were so unteachable") to the ideal, the perfect, the primordial ("from the beginning of creation"). The prohibition of divorce and remarriage also assumes a place in an overall worldview. It can be understood not as an interim ethic, nor as an ideal goal that will never be reached, but as a serious decree for a new age and a new order. Strenuous attempts have been made to portray Jesus's sayings about divorce and remarriage as tentative steps toward equality of the sexes. It has even been suggested, on the strength of Mark 10:12 that Jesus was advocating Roman law rather than Jewish principles. It is, of course, true that Jesus makes both sexes equal in the matter of divorce; but only because divorce and remarriage are denied equally to them both—on grounds wholly unconnected with sexual politics.

* * *

Similarity or dissimilarity? The fundamental divergence of scholars seeking to establish the authenticity of the various sayings of Jesus recorded in the New Testament involves more than at first appears. Those who argue that Jesus is best understood against the historical backdrop of first century Judaism, with its theological controversies and conflicting sects, will tend to agree that Jesus's message was essentially religious and probably millenarian. Those who seek to distance Jesus, for whatever reason, from the beliefs and mores of his day might at first seem to be asserting his divinity, his radical otherness, in a way that accords with orthodox Christian teaching. But that proves not to be the case. Instead they generally claim the opposite: that Jesus was at heart a social reformer whose gospel was one of radical change in religion and society. In line with Schweitzer's criticism of an earlier generation of Questers, they tend to portray a Jesus with their own interests and concerns: a post Enlightenment liberal Protestant with a contempt for the cultic, whose strong suit is egalitarianism and general liberation.

This divergence, moreover, proves in a strange way to be crucial in the argument about the ordination of women. Both sides in the women-priests debate have been eager to see Jesus as at variance with the mores of his day—in "advance" of them, they would probably say. On this point, as we have seen, the Vatican and the radical feminists are agreed. But that proves, on closer examination, to be an opinion based on no solid evidence whatever. It makes, moreover, little or no theological sense. Jesus the Jew, the hero of the latest phase in the on-going Quest, is far more convincing. Not only does he become historically intelligible—a figure in a landscape—but he finds his place in the great sweep of salvation history of which he is claimed to be the crisis and culmination. As the Jewish feminist scholar Judith Plaskow puts it:

> He is never portrayed as arguing for women's prerogatives, demanding changes in particular restrictive laws that affect women, or debating the Pharisees on the subject of gender . . . his relations to women and gender norms might not have been so different from the relations of his contemporaries.[18]

As Plaskow also points out, in a nation like Germany, with a long tradition of radical anti-Semitism, and a Reformation prejudice for seeing law and grace as competing opposites, the temptation for scholars to turn the Pharisees into fall guys and Jesus into the spokesperson for Aryan Protestantism, was obviously strong. But the doctrine of the Incarnation gives the lie to such speculation. The Jewishness of Jesus, absorbed with his mother's milk, is what made him who and what he is. A deracinated person is not exemplary: he is merely dysfunctional.

Supporters of women's ordination are prone to distinct but similar temptations: they have a consistent preference for the abstract and the generic over the individual and the particular. Canon Norris's famous paper talks about "the Christ" rather than "Jesus"; the Staggs called their study "Woman in the World of Jesus," and supposed that by analyzing his interaction with individual women they would learn something about his attitude to "womankind"; one writer expresses what has become a common

---

18. Plaskow, "Christian Feminism and Anti-Judaism," 307.

feminist view: "Jesus's sex—or Judaism or race or marital status or any fact of what he said or did in and of himself—is not relevant in confessing him as the Christ."

One can see only too clearly why feminists and their supporters would want to liberate Jesus from the context of Jewish patriarchy in which he lived and moved. But why should the Holy See, in documents of record, seek to do the same? The answer seems to lie in an institutional loss of nerve. The majestic panorama of Biblical history, once familiar to English readers from the Miltonic epics, *Paradise Lost* and *Paradise Regained*, has largely been displaced. In the words of Anthony Pagden:

> ... the Bible grants earthly history a single story line with an opening ("In the beginning"; the *fiat* of Creation), a catastrophe (the Fall), a crisis (the Incarnation and Resurrection of Christ), and an immanent end (the second coming of Christ as King, followed by "a new heaven and a new earth"), which will bring the tragedy of man to a happy ending (hence Dante's "divine *comedy*"). This historical drama, furthermore, had a heavenly Author: "I am the Alpha and the Omega, the beginning and the end, the first and the last."[19]

But in the modern West, that drama, even where it is still known, has largely lost credibility. The governing myth is now, not of Fall and Redemption, but of self-awareness and personal fulfillment. The existential question posed by the old story was: "How shall I be saved?" The leading question under the new dispensation is: "How can I be happy?" The first question expected a savior who would have authority. The only authority where the second question is concerned is necessarily the self. In the relativistic culture of competing ideologies which has largely replaced the Christian world view, Jesus is the one person, paradoxically, who can no longer be allowed to be himself: he has to be relevant. That is a principle which even the magisterium of the Catholic Church, it seems, feels obliged grudgingly to acknowledge.

* * *

So what did Jesus think about women? One is tempted to say that, in the sense of considering the status of women in the culture of his own day and in society at large, he did not think at all. The gospels give no indication whatever of any general reflection or sense of social purpose. There is no

19. Pagden, *Enlightenment: Why it still Matters*, 65.

evidence in them (or anywhere else in the New Testament) for a radical social program of what has been called "gender inclusivity." But arguments from silence are notoriously suspect. We need, then, to ask another question: was Jesus a misogynist? The accusation, about anyone, is often made on the slenderest of evidence: but apart from the occasional harsh word to or about his mother, there is surely too little evidence in Jesus's case to convict. He appears to have dealt with women much as he dealt with men, addressing their needs and their immediate predicament, showing respect for their common humanity. We have, of course, only the evangelists' word for any of this: as they edited the material much was no doubt omitted, and their own concerns, to a greater of lesser extent, came to the fore.

Christianity is an historical religion, not merely because it necessarily makes reference to a particular time and a particular person, but because all speculation and investigation about it is subject to the usual rules of historical probability. The Christian past is not prey to the ethical *a priori* assumptions of the present. It is what it was. The Quest for the historical Jesus has to some extent been displaced in recent scholarship by a quest for the earliest "christianities." There has been much talk of early Christian communities pioneering sexual egalitarianism—the deployment of women equally with men in leadership roles, as elders, prophets, and overseers. The question has to be where these communities, functioning in a world which is generally agreed to have been patriarchal and misogynistic, gained the courage and impetus to be so radically counter-cultural. The impetus must surely have come from Jesus: for to what other authority could they have appealed and what other authority would they have accepted? And yet it seems, that the New Testament writers, whose evidence is all that we have, did not find, record or even let slip any hint of corresponding sentiments in the sayings of the Master. The quest for the earliest Christianity is surely to a large extent dependent on the quest for the historical Jesus. A radical disconnect between the two is inconceivable because it is nonsensical. The great question which tormented scholars from Reimarus onwards was the question of how the gospel *about* Jesus related to the gospel *of* Jesus; of how the kerygma of the church related to the message of the kingdom. Some have supposed the relationship to be more tenuous than others. But all are agreed that there had to be a relationship. "Gender inclusivity" would have meant reversing the cultural norms both of the culture which gave Jesus birth and the society into which the church was born. How could Christians have embraced it, if they had no specific dominical authority for it—no word from the Lord?

3: Gentiles, Slaves, and Women

Paul avoids an abstract and unnatural perfection and makes perfection consist in the complete adjustment of spiritual and natural reality . . . That is the ideal of Paul's ethic, to live with the eyes fixed on eternity, while standing firmly on the solid ground of reality.

—ALBERT SCHWEITZER

If the Bible were a range of mountains I wonder what the mountain peak would be. I guess we probably have a different answer to this question every time we open the Bible. But certainly for me, one of the climatic passages—the one through which we then interpret many others—is this: Galatians 3:28 "There is no such thing as Jew and Greek, slave and free, male and female, for you are all one person in Jesus Christ." Now that great text—it has taken us in the Church a long while to work out what it means. The first bit "in Christ there is no Jew or Greek" only took us about 20 years or so to work out what it meant, and you can read about the debates and struggles the Church had over that text in the Bible itself. In the Acts of the Apostles and in some of Paul's letters you can see the Church grappling: "do you have to become a Jew before you can become a Christian—how does that work?" Well, we resolved it, though there were big disagreements. The next one, "there is no slave or free"—it took us 1,800 years to work that one out, but we did. Eventually we came to understand that in Christ there cannot be slavery, there cannot be slaves, we are all set free. And it falls to our generation to be those working out the full implications of "so what does it mean to say 'there is no male or female'?" We all agree it can make no difference to our baptism. We've sort of agreed and

found a way of living together by saying it shouldn't make any difference to someone being a priest. And now we say, should it affect
being a bishop as well?[1]

B ishop Stephen Cottrell's pitch for the ordination of women as bishops in the Church of England paints a grand historical picture: the
Whig view, one is tempted to say, of Christian history. The tide is advanc-
ing ever further up the beach of Progress, in an encouraging counter-
rhythm to Matthew Arnold's "melancholy, long, withdrawing roar." What
is Christianity *about*? It is about the freedom, dignity, and equality of the
individual. The argument is rhetorically powerful. From small beginnings
(Paul himself, it is claimed, was unable to grasp the full implications of his
own vision) the liberation of whole groups of people has progressed over
the years, gaining momentum in our own day, until the time has come to
surmount the final hurdle, to cross the last frontier. The pressure of history
is impelling us; we must not now be found wanting.

The argument is persuasive because it reiterates, in religious language,
the prevailing myth of the post-Enlightenment West. Roy Porter puts it
succinctly:

> Grand narratives . . . of how the West discovered and honed a
> distinctive self, unknown to earlier times, an inner, individualist
> psyche unfamiliar to the great civilisations of the East, underpin
> popular attitudes and public platitudes and continue to carry huge
> appeal.[2]

It is rhetorically powerful, but historically dubious. One gasps at the historical naiveté which attributes to the first century the ideas and achievements
of the eighteenth. The great achievements of the eighteenth century Enlightenment in the areas of religious toleration and human rights, however
they came about, were not the work of Christians. Nor could they plausibly
have been envisaged or prefigured by St. Paul. Whatever "in Christ there
is no such thing as Jew and Greek" meant to the Apostle (and we will return to that shortly), there can be no doubt about what, in terms of human
rights and liberties, it did not mean. It did not mean that Christians were
thenceforward obliged to accord ideological equivalence to their Jewish
neighbors. The seeds of religious toleration were sown not in the Christian

---

1. Text of a video issued in 2012 and available on the website of the Diocese of
Chelmsford.

2. Porter, R., *Flesh in the Age of Reason*, 12.

churches (and least of all in the Churches of the Reformation) but among the declared opponents of Christianity. Despite the heroic endeavors of English Evangelicals (and some Spanish and Portuguese Dominicans and Jesuits) in bringing it about, the demise of the Atlantic slave trade owed at least as much to the influence of the *philosophes* as it did to the Christian churches. Augustine and Aquinas both followed Aristotle and Cicero in defending the institution of slavery as a regrettable necessity, sanctioned by "nature," in a fallen world. Finally, to claim women's ordination as somehow the logical and inevitable conclusion of an unfolding program of Christian liberation is to confuse consequence and cause. The truth is that the churches are coming late to the table of sexual equality. The earliest campaigners for female rights paid little or no attention to women's ordination, simply because they supposed Christianity to be part of the problem and in no way part of the solution.

All this notwithstanding, the question persists: was Paul (as one writer has put it) "lobbing a verbal grenade at the established order of things . . . and he knew it?" We still need to ask whether so majestic a vision of expanding freedoms can reasonably be attributed to the Apostle. Did he really intend a wholesale revolution in religious and social attitudes? Indeed, did he suppose that the gospel which he preached was revolutionary at all, in any mundane sense of the word? Two things lead one to suspect not. In the first place, Paul is the man who had Timothy circumcised, sent Onesimus back to Philemon, and told the Corinthian women to go home and consult their husbands. And secondly, only one of the expanding freedoms supposedly catalogued in the Letter to the Galatians (and that a very doubtful proposition, as we will see) might be thought to have taken effect in his own lifetime. The others had to wait until the modern era. "It took 1,800 years to work that one out," as Cottrell disarmingly admits.

There is, moreover, another and more fundamental problem. It has become a commonplace that Paul was the founder, the inventor even, of Christianity. What began as an obscure chiliastic sect in a backwater of empire, it is said, Paul turned into a world religion with an expansive future. Viewed with the hindsight of Stephen Cottrell's millennia of development, there might appear to be some truth in the notion. But it is not how Paul would have seen it. Paul did nothing with an eye to a distant future, for the simple reason that he did not think there was one. Or rather, he thought that the future was out of his hands. Jesus, he believed, would soon return. Every sovereignty and power of this world would then be overthrown and be replaced by the reign of God and of his Christ. So familiar are we with that idea as rather extravagant poetic language (accompanied by the sonorous strains of George Frideric Handel) that we find it difficult to grasp as an imminent historical reality. Not so with Paul. He thought he knew what was going to happen, and he believed he had Jesus's word for it.

> We can tell you this from the Lord's own teaching, that any of us who are left alive until the Lord's coming will not have any advantage over those who have died. At the trumpet of God the voice of the archangel will call out the command and the Lord himself will come down from heaven: those who have died in Christ will be the first to rise and then those of us who are still alive will be taken up in the clouds together with them to meet the Lord in the air. So we shall stay with the Lord forever. With such thoughts as these you should comfort one another.[3]

From this belief consequences naturally followed. First, every disposition that Paul made for his infant churches was necessarily provisional: nothing could last. Secondly, he was obliged to pay scrupulous attention to the Lord's own instructions, because the time was at hand when he would be called to account. Paul's ordering of church life must always be read with those two factors in mind.

* * *

"The first bit 'in Christ there is no Jew or Greek' only took us about 20 years or so to work out what it meant, and you can read about the debates and struggles the Church had over that text in the Bible itself." But is it so simple? Does the New Testament paint so clear a picture? What did Jesus himself think about relations between Gentiles and Jews? Did Jesus envisage a Gentile mission? What was the belief and expectation of first century Jews about the inclusion of the Gentiles in the future Kingdom of God? And what was the nature of the disagreement between Paul and the leaders of the Jerusalem Church? Nothing, you can be sure, is as clear as at first it seems.

About Jesus there is very little evidence one way or the other. Whilst it is clearly stated that his own ministry was to the "lost sheep of the house of Israel," and though the disciples were told to restrict themselves to work among Jews (Matt 10:6), there are some incidents—like the meeting with the Syro-phoencian woman and the healing of the centurion's

---

3. 1 Thessalonians 4:15–19.

servant—which hint at a more "liberal" attitude than that of many of his contemporaries. All four evangelists, of course, were in favor of the Gentile mission (they wrote within and for it), but they place surprisingly little emphasis on it. In all probability there was a paucity of material in the tradition dealing with Jesus's attitude to, or work among, Gentiles—or they would have made a better job of commending a ministry to which they were themselves committed. Matthew makes the strongest case; but even there the issue is doubtful. Now because, for Jews, the subject was in the nature of things somewhat speculative (a vision for a perhaps distant future rather than an observation about the present), we cannot be sure what spectrum of opinion existed among Jesus's Jewish contemporaries. One thing, however, is certain: the focus of Jewish attention, then and thereafter, was on scrupulous observance of the Torah. W. D. Davies cites a number of examples which demonstrate that a wide range of theological viewpoints and opinions was tolerated, but that public *flouting* of the provisions of the Law resulted in condemnation and even death. Jesus himself was careful to respect the Torah.[4] E. P. Sanders points out that the Beatitudes, for example, do not abrogate the Law; they merely increase its stringency.[5] Paul was a self-declared Pharisee, zealous for the Law. "It is clear" writes W. L. Knox, "that Paul throughout his life continued to practice Judaism: and that he expected Jewish converts to do so."[6] "It is the seriousness with which the Apostle to the Gentiles still remained a Pharisee which is to be explained," wrote Davies.[7] Time and again the Acts of the Apostles reminds us that Paul invariably started his mission to a new city in its Synagogue. When he arrived in Rome, where there was already an established Christian community, it was not the Church which he called together, but the leaders of the Jewish community. Paul's Jewish punctiliousness moreover had the practical consequence that he could, on the strength of it, gain a hearing among fellow Jews, which would certainly not have been granted to an apparent apostate.

Something of a see-saw seems to have been taking place, in Rabbinic thinking, between the view that God's ultimate purpose was the inclusion of the Gentiles in his coming universal Kingdom (cf. Isa 49:6), and the idea that Israel's unique election as "my people" ensured that the twelve tribes

4. Davies, *Paul and Rabbinic Judaism*, 73.

5. Sanders, *Historical Figure of Jesus*, 201.

6. Knox, *St. Paul and the Church*, 112.

7. Davies, *Paul and Rabbinic Judaism*, 16.

would remain forever distinct and sacrosanct. Both views assumed without question that the Torah would continue to govern all the people of God. The same unresolved tensions can surely be found in Paul's thinking. No one who has carefully read the Letter to the Romans can possibly suppose that Paul had resolved the issue to his own or anyone else's satisfaction. Paul shared the internal conflicts that seem to have marked contemporary Judaism. He could not abandon a burning conviction about the election of Israel and the unique role of the Jewish nation in the mystery of salvation. Nor could he allow that the faith of his Gentile converts counted for nothing: the salvation of Jews somehow had to relate to Gentile faith in Jesus the Jewish Messiah. The imprecision was tolerable for one reason only: Paul's firm belief in an impending crisis which would end in the return of Jesus and the establishment of the reign of God. Paul passionately believed that the New Israel of the *parousia* would consist of those who were "in Christ"—both Jews and Greeks. It was a conviction rooted in a mysticism which allowed him to see all the baptized as members of Christ's risen body. In his own handwriting—to show his seriousness and exert his apostolic authority—he tells the Galatians:

> It does not matter if a person is circumcised or not; what matters is for him to become an altogether new creature. Peace and mercy to all who follow this rule, who form the Israel of God. I want no more trouble from anybody after this; the marks on my body are those of Jesus.[8]

But the *parousia* had not yet arrived. (Perhaps Paul's burning desire to preach the gospel in Spain, at the Pillars of Hercules—the very confines of the known world—was a campaign to bring it on.) The historical tension between Jew and Gentile remained, in consequence, a necessary part of present experience. By his own accidents of birth as both a Jew and a Roman citizen, Paul was inescapably a part of it. So, in the meantime, in this as in other things, Paul upheld the *status quo.* The circumcision of Timothy is thoroughly consistent with such a view.

Albert Schweitzer elevates this stasis into what he calls "a comprehensive theory." It runs: "Whatever was the external condition in which a man has made his election a reality, that is to say has become a believer, in that condition he is, as a believer, to remain."[9] This "theory of the *status quo*"

---

8. Galatians 6:15–18.

9. Schweitzer and Montgomery, *Mysticism of Paul the Apostle,* 194.

is closely related to Schweitzter's view of Paul's mystical eschatology; but it is not necessary to buy the whole Schweitzer package to see that he has a point. The "theory" can as well be explained by Paul's distinctive take on what was, after all, current Rabbinic doctrine. The coming of the Messiah, it was believed, would bring a "new law," not in the sense of the abrogation of the old, but its extension and more prefect interpretation. Paul had come to see that, in Jesus, what was expected had already come to pass. In view of that fact, he had come to believe that loyalty to the new Law of Christ did not involve any disloyalty to the old. There was, in consequence, no inconsistency in maintaining that Gentiles need not be inaugurated into the Jewish community (by circumcision and subjection to the ceremonial Torah), but that he himself must show his identification with Israel "according to the flesh" by his strict and unvarying observance. He was thereby being true both to the "new" and to the "old" Israel.

It "only took us about 20 years or so to work out what it meant," says Cottrell. If by "us" and by "working out what it meant," he means the establishment of an overwhelmingly Gentile church in which Jewish ritual regulations no longer applied, then it took much longer than twenty years, and was not, in any case, part of the Pauline project. Paul, it needs once more to be emphasized, could not have intended it, since his most passionate belief was in another and more spectacular outcome. The compromise reached at the so-called Council of Jerusalem (if that is the "us" to which Cottrell is referring) became largely irrelevant with the virtual annihilation of Palestinian Christianity following Titus's campaign of AD 70. It never recovered. And the personal tensions with which Paul wrestled in the Letter to the Romans died with it. The provisions of the Jerusalem compromise, however—not eating meat sacrificed to idols and abstaining from blood—were upheld by Paul in his lifetime and continued to be observed by Christians for several centuries afterwards, despite the considerable inconvenience. These minimum demands of the Jewish Law were by no means trivial. There was a close connection in most ancient cities between the cult of the gods and the meat trade. The Jerusalem regulations must have made table fellowship between Christians and pagans virtually impossible, and the purchase of meat, in all but the most regulated circumstances, a hazardous proceeding. It was more likely than not that a Christian out to supper with pagan friends would have something forbidden offered him. Tertullian (c,160–c.225) claims that pagans used to test Christians by tempting them to eat black pudding.[10] History and atrophy, then, not egalitarian ideology, finally settled the matter.

* * *

The position of slaves in the Pauline churches has been the subject of much debate. It will be as well to begin by saying something generally about slavery in first century Rome. Slaves were numerous, probably about 30 percent of the population in first century Italy, though perhaps less in the rest of the Empire. Slavery was not racially based; slaves were drawn from all over Europe and the Mediterranean, including Celts, Germans, Thracians, Greeks, Carthaginians, and a small group of Ethiopians in Roman Egypt. By the first century BC, custom precluded the enslavement of Roman citizens and Italians living in Gallia Cisalpina, but previously many southern and central Italians had been enslaved after defeat. Slaves in Italy were mainly indigenous Italians. Roman slaves could own property, and there was a wide divergence of status, wealth, and education within the slave community. The elite among the slaves, the so-called *familia Caesaris* (household of the emperor), formed an imperial civil service which grew in size and influence until curbed by Hadrian. It was not uncommon for high-ranking slaves to marry free women. Slaves could earn money and retain it; some earned enough to buy their own freedom; a small number ended their lives as not inconsiderable property owners. None of this, however, should be allowed to cloud the fact that slaves were an oppressed minority, at the bottom of a social order with little inbuilt mobility. Judging from the literature of the time, freedmen were the butt of snobbish humor. Trimalchio, in *The Golden Ass,* is one such. No religious cult or philosophical group in the ancient world opposed slavery, though the mystery religions (and in particular Mithraism) admitted slaves among their adepts. Paul hailed from Tarsus, a considerable Mithraic center.[11] It should be added that, as a Roman citizen, he came from a class which could not, for any reason, be enslaved.

"Christianity is a religion of slaves, children, and women,"[12] runs the old saw; but how many slaves, proportionally, were there in Paul's churches? And what was Paul's attitude to them, and to slavery as an institution? It is impossible to estimate numbers with any accuracy. There were certainly

10. Tertullian, *Apologeticum,* 9, 13–14.

11. Cumont, *Mysteries of Mithra.*

12. Origen, *Contra Celsum,* book 4.

both slaves and slave owners in the Pauline churches. "Chloe's people" (1 Cor 1:11) were quite possibly household slaves and there would certainly have been slaves among those of the "household of Caesar" who joined Paul in sending greetings to the Philippians (Phil 4:22). It would be easy, on the strength of Celsus's classic put-down, to exaggerate. In the second century, however, Christian groups were still characterized by an inclusive membership of differing classes and conditions. This was seen by contemporaries as quite different from the largely self-selecting and monochrome sodalities of various kinds, religious and secular, which proliferated in most of the cities of the Empire. In 1 Corinthians 7:20–24, in the course of an exposition on marriage, divorce, and celibacy, Paul addresses a slave rhetorically. The apparently casual reference alerts us to two things: that there were slaves (or at least a slave!) in Paul's audience (it would be a strange example to choose if there were not), and that there was no embarrassment in making such a casual reference (as there might well be in a modern audience if the reference were to blacks or Pakistanis). Apparently Paul and his audience were at home with slavery, both as a fact and as a concept.

Albert Schweitzer's prime exhibit in defending his "theory of the *status quo*" is, of course, the letter to Philemon. That letter shows Paul at his most winning and gracious; but it falls far short of demanding, or even recommending, the manumission of Onesimus. It should be read as a practical outworking of the principles laid down in 1 Corinthians.

> Let everyone stay as he was at the time of his call. If when you were called you were a slave do not let this bother you; even if you could become free, rather remain as you are. A slave, when he is called in the Lord, becomes the Lord's freedman, and a freedman called in the Lord becomes Christ's slave. You have all been bought and paid for; do not be slaves of other men. Each one of you, my brothers, should stay as he was before God at the time of his call.[13]

The whole letter to Philemon is a similar pattern of paradoxes. Paul is a slave: he is in chains for Jesus, chains which he has willingly accepted. Onesimus is a slave, but unwillingly: he has run away from his captivity. In doing so he has providentially stumbled upon Paul, who converts him, sets him free in Christ, and calls him his son. Philemon, on the other hand, is a free man who owns slaves. He has been converted by Paul, and so, like Onesimus, he is Paul's son in the faith and a slave of Christ. The debt Philemon owes to Paul is incalculable—the debt of his salvation. Paul graciously points out

13. 1 Corinthians 7:20–22.

that (unbeknownst to Philemon) Onesimus has been discharging that debt of gratitude on Philemon's behalf by his service to Paul. It is now time for all debts to be paid in full, and Paul's two converts to be reconciled. Probably some additional financial issue clouds the past history of slave and slave owner—"it is possible that a theft, as the cause of the running away, may be in question," says Schweitzer.[14] Paul graciously offers to pay any sum outstanding in order to facilitate the reconciliation. At the same time he tactfully reminds Philemon that he owes him everything. Then comes the dénouement. Paul (the slave) sends Onesimus (the slave) back to Philemon (the master), whilst reminding Philemon that both are "sons" of Paul, and all are slaves of Christ. They were bought at a price, and are now enthralled to the real Master. They must therefore imitate Christ as Paul is doing: relationships are to be transformed, debts are to be discharged in love, and the gospel is to be realized in lives of obedience. Onesimus and Philemon are to live according to the pattern set out in the hymn which Paul, from his prison, once quoted to his Philippians:

> In your minds you must be the same as Christ Jesus. His state was divine, yet he did not cling to his equality with God, but emptied himself to assume the condition of a slave, and became as men are. And being as all men are, he was humbler yet, even to accepting death, death on a cross.[15]

The Letter to Philemon is more than clever rhetorical use of paradox (though it is certainly that). It reveals Paul to us in a unique way. "Paul," says Schweitzer again, "is the only man of Primitive-Christian times whom we really know, and he is a man of profound and admirable humanity." In a characteristically purple passage, he goes on:

> Side by side with Paul's achievement as a thinker must be set his achievement as a man. Having a personality at once simple and profound, he avoids an abstract and unnatural perfection and makes perfection consist in the complete adjustment of spiritual and natural reality . . . That is the ideal of Paul's ethic, to live with the eyes fixed on eternity, while standing firmly on the solid ground of reality.[16]

---

14. Schweitzer and Montgomery, *Mysticism of Paul the Apostle*, 331.

15. Philemon 2:5–8

16. Schweitzer and Montgomery, *Mysticism of Paul the Apostle*, 331.

Here surely is the nub of the matter. How can one imagine Paul seeking to demolish an institution that provided him with so lively and poignant an image of the Gospel life of obedience, submission, and mutual forbearance? He was, as he repeatedly points out, living that life himself. It is possible to criticize Paul, as many have done, for his failure, despite his profound human sympathy, to condemn slavery as an institution. But that is rather to miss the point. The transformation of the world in which he is engaged, under the pressure of the impending eschaton, both accepts the here-and-now and infinitely transcends it. "There must be no passing of premature judgement," he tells the Corinthians, "Leave that until the Lord comes; He will light up all that is hidden in the dark and reveal the secret intentions of men's hearts."[17] The trick, then, is to be free in slavery, and to know oneself still a slave when free: to embrace values which, because they are other-worldly, transform the world. Jesus, whose service is perfect freedom, will resolve all at his coming. There is something tragic in the notion of accusing Paul for not campaigning for "the rights of man and of the citizen." It is not merely an anachronism, it is an insult. Paul commends a degree of patience and compassion of which the most ardent abolitionist might yet remain incapable. Paul was aiming not at social justice, but at sanctity. However much we may admire Condorcet, Diderot, and Rousseau (and despite Voltaire's entombment in the Pantheon), they were none of them saints. It may be that their greatest achievement lay in supressing the hidden Robespierre in each one of them.

* * *

At the end of a lengthy passage on prophecy and speaking in tongues (and before he goes on to his great hymn on the Resurrection of the Body in chapter 15), Paul gives his Corinthian correspondents specific directions about the conduct of public worship:

> As in all the churches of the saints, the women should keep silence in the churches. For they are not permitted to speak but should be subordinate, as even the law says. If there is anything that they desire to know, let them ask their husbands at home. For it is shameful for a woman to speak in church. What! Did the word of God originate with you, or are you the only ones it has reached? If anyone thinks he is a prophet, or spiritual, he should acknowledge

17. 1 Corinthians 4:5.

that what I am writing to you is a command from the Lord. If anyone does not recognize this he is not recognized. So, my brethren, earnestly desire to prophesy, and so not forbid speaking in tongues; but all things should be done decently and in order.[18]

It is easy, if one has the will, to make heavy weather of the interpretation of this passage; but it is not the insoluble conundrum that some have hoped to make of it. Nor is this plausibly a later interpolation—a view that is losing ground among commentators. On the contrary, the argument here fits neatly into the developing pattern of Paul's thought, and has distinctly Pauline characteristics.

The key to understanding Paul's argument is the distinction he is making between two sorts of speaking: *lalein glosse* (speaking in tongues), which he associates closely with prophecy, and *lalein en ekklesia* (speaking in the assembly). The first, Paul has already made clear to his Corinthians (11:5ff.), is permitted to women. The second he forbids to women with as firm and categorical a series of injunctions as any in the Pauline corpus. It is a commonplace among commentators that Paul's theology is occasional (that is to say, directed to a particular audience and need), rather than systematic. But the careful reader soon observes in Paul's habitual patterns of argument something which, whilst it is not systematic theology, certainly approaches it. Paul habitually argues on different levels of authority; and so a useful tool in understanding his pattern of thought is a list of those levels in ascending order of importance or seriousness. They are five:

1. The general moral code—patterns of behaviour which are thought, by society at large, to be "natural" or unchallengeable.

2. Paul's own authority as an apostle and founder of churches.

3. The general practice of the Christian churches.

4. The principles of the Jewish Torah.

5. A command of the Lord Jesus Christ.

These levels of authority are sometimes invoked in isolation from each other. Sometimes, however, they are made to work together, as we see at 1 Corinthians 9:1–14, where Paul is demonstrating that he is entitled to financial support for his labors, and that he has freely renounced it. Paul begins by appealing to the common practice of other Christian communities (our level 3—"as the other apostles, and the brothers of the Lord and Cephas"

18. 1 Corinthians 14:33b–40, Jerusalem Bible.

[v. 5]). He goes on to talk in more general terms (our level 1—"who serves as a soldier at his own expense, who plants a vineyard without eating any of its fruit?" [v. 7]). At a more serious level (our level 4) he appeals to the authority of the Torah ("does not the law say the same?" [v. 8]). His ultimate sanction, (which for Paul and no doubt his readers settles the matter, is our level 5—the claim to have a word from the Lord himself on the subject ("in the same way the Lord commanded." [v. 14]).

The same levels of authority are used here to forbid women to "speak in the assembly." Paul has been giving a whole series of instructions about day-to-day church matters referred to him by the Corinthian PCC. In general they are directions made on apostolic authority alone (our level 3): "Be imitators of me as I am of Christ." The instructions about veils and hairdressing, numbers of speakers, and the availability of interpreters are all of this kind. Now he brings out his big guns. Not Paul's opinion alone, but the universal practice of the churches (level 3) "as in all the assemblies of the saints"; "did the word of God originate with you, or are you the only ones it has reached?"; the Torah itself (level 4)—"as even the law says"; and finally, the Lord in person (level 5)—"what I am writing to you is a command of the Lord"—are the authority by which he speaks. Then, as though this apparent authoritarian overkill were not enough (and as an eloquent testimony to the intransigence and willfulness of the Corinthians), he adds the threat of formal anathema—"if anyone does not recognize this, he is not recognized." (The reference is to the saying we have recorded at Matthew 7:21–23: "Many will say to me in that day, Lord, Lord . . . then I will say to them: I never knew you, depart from me you workers of iniquity"; cf. "if anyone has no love for the Lord, let him be accursed" (1 Cor 16:22), with which, in his own hand, Paul ends the present letter.)

There can be no reasonable doubt, considering the weight of the language used, that Paul is absolutely serious in forbidding women to "speak in the assembly." For faithful Christians, then, it is a matter of importance to decide what he means by that phrase. Could "speaking in the assembly" conceivably have been a technical term familiar, no doubt, to Paul's readers but obscure to us? There are substantial reasons for supposing this to be the case. The distinction between *lalein glosse* and *lalein en ekklesia* is between a charismatic and a formally ordered ministry. Such a distinction the Jews had themselves already been making for centuries. *Lalein glosse* (speaking in tongues), like the wider category of "prophecy," is a province open to women as well as men. "As even the law says," the Spirit moves whom it will, men and women, adults and children. Though Paul was of the opinion that in public such things should be ordered and regulated, he accepted all this as a matter of fact. A tradition extending from Miriam to Anna was one which a pupil of Gamaliel could be expected to take for granted. *Lalein in ekklesia* (speaking in the assembly) is obviously something quite different. We know that simply because Paul can restrict it to men on the same principles ("as even the law says.") which permitted women to prophesy. The entire liturgical activity of Israel, in both temple and synagogue, was restricted to males. But, in this particular context, what "law" forbids what activity?

Fruitless hours of research have been expended trying to find a passage in the Pentateuch to which Paul could conceivably be referring. The truth seems to be that Paul is not using "*nomos*" in the narrow sense of the Pentateuch, but in the broader sense of Holy Tradition: Mishnah, not scripture. (Neither, of course, existed in Paul's day in the form in which we know them). There are two relevant proscriptions in the rabbinic tradition. The first forbids women to take part in the public question-and-answer sessions which were the foundations of rabbinic discourse. A woman, says Rabbi Eliezer, had better do her arguing with her husband privately. ("If there is anything they desire to know, let them ask their husbands at home," says Paul, echoing him.) The second forbids a woman to preside at the Passover meal. The Passover Haggadah includes questions asked of the eldest present by the youngest. Could a dowager, the eldest in her household, be the required respondent? The Rabbis held that she could not. She had better unite her household to that of her nearest male kinsman so that the obligations of the festival could be fulfilled by a male on her behalf.

If we assume—and we have no reason not to assume—that the earliest churches borrowed the "dialogue sermon" from Jewish custom, we have here two restrictions which cover neatly the role of the celebrant at the Christian eucharist. He is, in Jewish terms, both the Rabbi teaching formally (*dialegesthai* is the verb used in Acts 20:7) and the elder (*presbyteros*) who heads the table at the Paschal celebration (the role which Paul himself assumed after that near-fatal dialogue sermon in Troas). Precisely because the charismatic ministries of the Corinthian community were so lively as to be a cause for concern (and because women, as the law permitted, were active in them), Paul needed to use all the authority at his disposal to make the necessary distinction between such extraordinary gifts and the rather more mundane, formally sanctioned, ministry of the *presbyteroi*, from which he knew women to be excluded by a specific dictum of the Savior.

It has been suggested that by "a command of the Lord" Paul means some word of his own, speaking with the apostolic authority of an "ambassador of the Lord Jesus Christ." But this cannot be. Already, he has written: "to the married I give charge, not I but the Lord . . . to the rest I say, not the Lord." And again: "Now concerning virgins I have no command from the Lord, but I give my opinion as one who by the Lord's mercy is trustworthy."[19] Far from his being casual about the distinction, it would seem that, in Paul's opinion, confusion about the source and nature of spiritual authority is the real problem at Corinth. He is therefore assiduous in pointing it up. *Entole* (command), moreover, designates, not a general principle, from which Paul might be thought to have adduced a particular directive of his own, but a specific "precept," an actual "word." Here, then, a specific command (*entole*) of the Lord Jesus is being used as evidence that the general principles of the Law, as they apply in the changed circumstances of Christian worship, still hold good. The teaching role and the table presidency of the Church are a male preserve. The Lord, Paul is telling a Corinthian community intoxicated with novelty, willed no change.

* * *

Gentiles, slaves, and women: there seems to be little or no evidence that the Paul who wrote Galatians 3:28 sought radical changes in the status of any of them, either within the churches or in the ambient society. His infant churches had problems peculiarly their own. Even if he had thought it desirable, he must have concluded that a wider program of social engineering would be impractical. But it was not merely pragmatism (or eschatology!) that determined his stance. There is ample evidence that Paul was by upbringing and temperament what would nowadays be called a social conservative. One of the governing images of his theology—that of the church as a body—had a long history in political conservatism before the Apostle adapted it to his needs. From Greek antiquity to Shakespeare's *Coriolanus* the image has been employed to support notions of a stratified, hierarchical society in which everyone knows his or her place.

In an extended footnote, John Robinson[20] cites no less an authority than Michael Ramsey for the view that the use of *soma* to mean a group of people was "quite unfamiliar, if not entirely unknown to the people to

19. 1 Corinthians 7:10–12

20. Robinson, J. A. T., *The Body: Study in Pauline Theology*, 48–49.

whom Paul was writing." Robinson goes on to mitigate this claim with a number of examples to the contrary. As well he might. For the earliest use of the image of which we have record—in the Rig-Veda, a collection of Sanskrit hymns that is the oldest religious text of the Hindus—already has a social and "political" connotation. It is an account of the gods sacrificing Purusa (the archetype of mortal man or the human race personified) and creating different social classes from the parts of his body:

> The Brahman [priests] was his mouth, of both arms was the Rajanya [warriors] made. His thighs became the Vaisya [shepherds], from his feet were the Sudra [servants] made.[21]

The Rig-Veda is usually dated from around 1500 BC; but there are reasons for supposing that the hymn in question is later, say around 550 BC. From that time the image seems to have seeped into the collective Indo-European sub-conscious. It resurfaces in more familiar territory in the fable of the Belly and the Members, which scholars have assumed to have been added to the Aesop canon rather later than most of the rest of the collection. In the written version of the fable, the Hands and Feet denounce the Belly for eating everything and doing nothing, and refuse to give it any more food with the result that they waste away till they are too weak to feed the Belly even if they want to. The story emerges again, transmuted by circumstance and usage, in Livy's history of Rome (written during the first few years of the Christian era). Livy tells how, when the Plebs defected from Rome in the early years of the Republic, the Patricians sent one Menenius Agrippa to persuade them to return. It is the passage made famous by its inclusion in *Coriolanus*. In Livy (and in Plutarch), Menenius's recitation quells the rebellion. Not so in Shakespeare, where the citizens know more than one version of the story, and turn it against Menenius. The image of society as a "body," though it may, as Ramsey claimed, be absent from "the Christian literature . . . the Septuagint . . . or the papyri," seems nevertheless to have become a commonplace by Paul's time. Aesop, after all, was part of popular culture. Socrates, during his imprisonment, set himself the task of producing a verse adaptation "because they were stories I knew and had handy"—that is, he knew them by heart. The image, moreover, had always had inescapable political connotations. Its roots, as we have seen, lie in the caste system.

21. *Rig-Veda X, hymn 90*, in Clayton, *Rig-Veda and Vedic Religion*, 166.

It is clear, moreover, that the idea was not new to Paul's readers. Nowhere does he feel the need to explain it. But for Paul it is more than a figure of speech. The Pauline use of the image is obviously quite different from the notion of social hierarchy found in Plato and later in Cicero. The "Golden Lie" which Plato proposed should be deployed in the education of a virtuous elite, is an allegorical account of a fixed hierarchy of talent. We are to think of souls as bronze, silver, and golden; the bronze souls are the workers, the silver are the soldiers ("auxiliaries" in Plato's terminology), and the golden are the guardians, the philosopher kings. Plato even devotes considerable attention to arrangements which will ensure that elite parents breed elite children! Paul's "body," on the other hand, is organic and actual, not mineral and allegorical, dynamic and not static. Nowhere, it should be noted, does Paul say that the Church is *like* a body: it *is* a body, the body of the Risen Christ. The "mystical" use of such language is part of Paul's comprehensive overview of salvation history. The Church is the body of Jesus, and so proleptically it is a manifestation of the coming kingdom. It will one day be a "glorious" body, revealed as the resurrection body it is in process of becoming. When Christ is revealed, all mundane distinctions of status, race, and sex will be irrelevant since all will be one in their relation to the Father in his Son. That, not Cottrell's sweeping program of social reform, is the true import of Gal 3:28, 1 Cor 12:13, and Col 3:11. In present rather than eschatological time, Christ's body the Church is nevertheless related structurally to existing social patterns. There is, admittedly, a degree of utopian optimism in his conviction that the different parts of the body will accept their allotted function and rejoice in it. But *la carrière ouverte aux talents* there most certainly is not.

This anchoring of eschatological hope in present realities is seen again in what for many theologians, from Augustine to Luther, was one of the most characteristic Pauline doctrines: that of obedience to lawful authority. This is no place to go into later developments of Romans 13—though it is worth remarking that none of the later developments of the doctrine of non-resistance has proved attractive to modern liberals. Suffice it to say that the clue to understanding Paul's position is again to be found in his eschatology. "Besides, you know, 'the time' has come: you must wake up now. Our salvation is even nearer than it was when we were converted."[22] Secular authority is to be respected and obeyed not merely on pragmatic grounds (the infant church needed to avoid unnecessary persecution in or-

22. Romans 13:11.

der to thrive), but because the secular authorities are a dispensation of the Divine Providence. And because the ultimate authority which lies behind them is imminent and will, when he comes, vindicate the elect.

* * *

We began this chapter with the Bishop of Chelmsford's claim that Galatians 3:28 is a pivotal text in understanding Paul, and much of the rest of scripture—that it is "the one through which we then interpret many others." That is a bold claim; and one which stands in a long tradition. Since the end of the seventeenth century, liberal Christians have been engaged in a self-defeating program of assimilating the content of the scriptures to the insights of the Enlightenment. The presuppositions of a post-Christian—often anti-Christian—culture have been imposed upon authors who were ignorant of them, and whose own presuppositions were radically different. This has generally resulted in absurdities, like the eighteenth century attempts (not least that of Thomas Jefferson) to excise from the New Testament all elements of the miraculous. It is a program that continues to captivate the vulgar imagination. But with the benefit of hindsight we can see that such attempts are simply a failure of historical imagination—a failure to grasp that truths which seemed self-evident in 1776 were simply unthinkable seventeen centuries before. There is more to this than historical myopia, however. It is a process which renders those who engage in it insensitive to the real values and insights of the past. The authentic voice of Paul is drowned out by current concerns, and perhaps the greatest thinker in the long history of Christianity is reduced to a mere adjunct of modern liberal cliché.

4: Alas, Poor Andronicus!

I am all the daughters of my Father's house and all the brothers too.

—*TWELFTH NIGHT*, ACT 2, SCENE 4

At the very end of the Letter to the Romans, Paul sends personal greetings to a group of acquaintances now resident in the city:

> I commend to you our sister Phoebe, a deaconess of the church at Cenchreae. Give her, in union with the Lord, a welcome worthy of saints, and help her with anything she needs: she has looked after a great many people, myself included.
>
> My greetings to Prisca and Aquila, my fellow workers in Christ Jesus, who risked death to save my life: I am not the only one to owe them a debt of gratitude, all the churches among the pagans do as well. My greetings also to the church that meets at their house.
>
> Greetings to my friend Epaenetus, the first of Asia's gifts to Christ; greetings to Mary who worked so hard for you; to those outstanding apostles Andronicus and Junias, my compatriots and fellow prisoners who became Christians before me; to Ampliatus, my friend in the Lord; to Urban, my fellow worker in Christ; to my friend Stachys; to Apelles who has gone through so much for Christ; to everyone who belongs to the household of Aristobulus; to my compatriot Herodion; to those in the household of Narcissus who belong to the Lord; to Tryphaena and Tryphosa, who work hard for the Lord; to my friend Persis who has done so much for the Lord; to Rufus, a chosen servant of the Lord, and to his mother who has been a mother to me too. Greetings to Asyncritus, Phlegon, Hermes, Patrobas, Hermas, and all the brothers who

are with them; to Philologus and Julia, Nereus and his sister, and
Olympas and all the saints who are with them. Greet each other
with a holy kiss. All the churches of Christ send greetings.[1]

They are a motley crew, whose only common features seem to be their association with Paul and their enthusiasm for the gospel. The list tells us a
good deal about the composition and disposition of the Pauline churches.
Early Christianity, it seems, was a close-knit family affair, even in the capital. In all, twenty-nine people are cited and twenty-seven named. Among
them there are four (possibly five) married couples, a brother and sister,
and a mother and son. There are four (possibly five) households or *eccle-
siae domesticae*, (probably including slaves). Andronicus and Junia/s and
Herodion are described as Paul's relations or compatriots, and like him they
have been imprisoned for the faith. The picture, then, is of an essentially
domestic church. All those mentioned have distinguished themselves in
their service of the Gospel and in some cases been of personal assistance to
Paul himself. The bonds are close and perhaps, emotional. Prisca (Priscilla)
and Aquila had somehow been responsible for Paul's very survival. Aquila,
like Paul, was a Jew (as some of the others probably were), and had the same
profession: he was a tent maker. First century Rome was a city of between
one and two million people. Like a majority of the inhabitants of the city,
all of these were probably immigrants. Phoebe is making a first appearance from Cenchrae. Prisca and Aquila (who came from Pontus on the
Black Sea) were seasoned travelers: they hove up in Ephesus and Corinth
as well as Rome. Epaenetus originated from somewhere in Asia Minor.
John Chrysostom gives a full, if rather rhetorical account in the thirtieth
chapter of his homilies on Romans. Somewhat predictably, the sparseness
of information about them, as with other named characters in the early
church, has led to a good deal of airy speculation. Marcus Borg and John
Dominic Crossan were convinced that it was Phoebe who took Paul's letter
to Rome.[2] Adolf Harnack surmised that Prisca and Aquila were joint authors of the Letter to the Hebrews.[3] And Junia/s has become an industry
in her own right.

First there is the fairly basic question of sex. Was the Junia/s referred
to by Paul at Romans 16:7 male or female? Whole books have been written

1. Romans 16:1–16, Jerusalem Bible.

2. Borg and Crossan, *The First Paul*, 51.

3. Harnack, *Ueber die beiden Recensionen*, 2–13.

to prove she was a woman.[4] But the evidence is the reverse of conclusive. Everything turns upon accents in the Greek, which (though they had been invented by the time of Paul) were not used in the earliest texts of the New Testament. Jounian ('Ἰουνίαν) is the spelling of the name for both sexes. Add an acute accent over the "I" and the name is female (Junia), add a circumflex over the "a" and the name is male (Junias). There are no further clues from the gender of the surrounding words, since in Greek grammar they are governed by the presence of "Andronicus," an undoubted male. When, in the ninth century, the Greek text came habitually to be written with accents, the overwhelming majority of manuscripts opted for the masculine form. But that, say the Junia enthusiasts, is no more than further evidence of monkish misogyny, and in any case, the male form of the name is almost unknown in first century texts.[5] Patristic evidence does not really help either. Jerome (c. 345–420) read "Julia," a rare textual variant. Epiphanius of Salamis (315–403) says that "Junias, of whom Paul makes mention, became Bishop of Apamneia in Syria," so he was a man. Origen, in his commentary on Romans (admittedly surviving only in a Latin translation), has the male form too. The champion of Junia is John Chrysostom (347–407), whose commentary on Romans is fulsome in her praise: "O how great is the devotion of this woman that she should be counted worthy of the appellation of an apostle!"[6] (It is an undoubted compliment; though an ardent feminist might find it a little backhanded.) So was Junia/s a man or a woman? The only answer that can confidently be given to a question which has generated a mountain of paper and endless speculation in the blogosphere is that (taking full account of modern understandings of intersex biology) s/he was most probably one or the other.

Then there is the question of the job description. Did Paul ever say that Junia/s—male or female—was an apostle? And if so, what did he mean? Though all the people mentioned by Paul at the end of Romans were no doubt prominent in their local Christian communities (as well as being his close friends), only three of them seem to have had what we would now call an "office" in the church: Phoebe is "diakonos" and "prostatis," Andronicus and Junia/s (husband and wife; brother and sister; brothers; inseparable friends?) may have been "apostles." We can conclude that the Roman Church to which Paul was writing was largely unstructured,

4. Epp, *Junia: First Woman Apostle*.

5. Ibid., 67.

6. Chrysostom, *Homily on Epistle to the Romans*, cap. XXX, ver. 7.

unhierarchical, and probably quite fluid in its organization. The question then arises: what precisely might be meant by calling Phoebe a deacon and Andronicus and Junia/s apostles? The first mistake to avoid is supposing the terms bear any direct relation to the orders of the church in later, more settled times. They are probably best understood as functional rather than hierarchical. A "deacon" is "one who serves" (cf. Mark 1:31—"she began to wait on them" and Acts 6:2—"to serve tables"). This reading is borne out by the parallel use of "prostatis," which the NAS New Testament Greek Lexicon translates as "a female guardian, protectress, patroness, caring for the affairs of others and aiding them with their resources" (cf. Luke 8:2–3—"several other [women] who provided for them out of their resources"). "Apostolos," you will remember, is a term with an eventful history, extending from the mercantile marine to the early church. Suffice it to say that it is very loosely used in the Pauline letters: Epaphroditus (Phil 2:25), for example, seems to be so-called on the strength of his carrying out an embassy on behalf of the Philippians; Apollos (1 Cor 4:6–9) is simply named from his association with Paul and his mission. Strange, then, that scholars usually noted for their skepticism and their reluctance to concede the New Testament roots of the three-fold ministry, develop a sudden access of credulity when it comes to women. "Diakonos" and "prostatis" have been readily equated, by North American evangelicals, with notions of church "leadership."[7] And for catholic-minded Anglicans in favor of women's ordination, "apostle" has elided easily into "bishop." Most of this, of course, is mere wishful thinking, carried forward on the slenderest evidence. But it is at this point that the putative Junia comes into her own. Suddenly, in one daring leap of faith we are all the way from a one-liner at the end of the letter to the Romans to a wholesale revision of the orders of the universal church. Enthusiasts have not only been willing to jump through all the hoops: they seem blissfully unaware of the absurdity of doing so.

The fact is that, whatever Paul might have meant by "apostle," it is by no means certain he applied the term to Junia/s. The operative phrase is *episemoi en toi apostoloi*, "well-known as apostles" or "well-known to (or by) the apostles"; "prominent among" or "familiar to." Between Eldon Epp[8] and Burer and Wallace,[9] the controversy has raged to no very

---

7. See Payne, *Man and Woman: One in Christ.*

8. Epp, "Text-critical, Exegetical, and Socio-cultural," 267ff.

9. Burer and Wallace, "Was Junia Really an Apostle," 76–79.

satisfactory conclusion. Both uses of *en* + dative seem to be attested in early texts. Which one applies here remains anybody's guess.

* * *

It is to this doubtful, ramshackle edifice that Richard Bauckham has attached his startlingly baroque extension. A prize-winning former Professor of New Testament Studies in the University of St. Andrews, Bauckham has single-handedly done for his "Joanna/Junia" what it took centuries of impacted legend to accomplish for the Magdalen. On the strength of two references in Luke's gospel and a tendentious reading of the letter to the Romans, he translates her from Galilee to Rome and has made of her a founding mother of the local church. "No historical reconstruction is possible without the exercise of imagination," he rightly says, echoing Elizabeth Schüssler Fiorenza.[10] But here we have imagination run riot. Passages of numbing erudition are linked by wild and unsupportable speculation. ". . . we cannot exclude the possibility . . ."; ". . . it is plausible . . ."; ". . . may well have . . ."; ". . . cannot be ruled out . . ." The text is littered with hypotheses, and the conclusion of it all is a "reconstruction" which reads like a prospectus for twentieth century liberal Christianity.

> Joanna knew that Jesus was no mere charismatic healer, but that his healings were integral to a vision of the coming kingdom of God. Her own healing brought her into growing participation in this vision, which included an un-compromising call to repentance, a corresponding enactment of God's transformative forgiveness, and the inclusion of all kinds of marginal and excluded people in the Jewish people of God as Jesus was beginning to reconstitute it. Jesus' practice of the coming kingdom drew together a community of disciples among whom the life of the kingdom was taking form in the renunciation of all status and wealth. This was the particular challenge for Joanna, who could have remained, as others did, a sympathizer with Jesus' movement without leaving her home and social location. But Joanna took the step of disciple-ship, for her a step across the whole of the social gulf that separated the Tiberian elite from the ordinary people, not to mention the beggars, the prostitutes, and other outcasts with whom Jesus habitually associated. But she herself was an outcast of a sort, one of the oppressors, in her identification with Rome and its Herodian clients a traitor

---

10. Bauckham, *Gospel Women*, 194.

to the Jewish national and religious cause. Throwing in her lot with Jesus was a radical conversion to the poor, but it must have been the nondiscriminating acceptance with which the community of Jesus' disciples welcomed all who joined them, even tax collectors, that gave her the confidence to risk her reputation among her peers, burning her bridges behind her, in order to identify herself as fully as possible with Jesus and his movement. Among these people, her status brought her no honor; not even her substantial donations to the common fund gave her a place above others. But instead she found a place in what Jesus called his new family of those who were practicing the will of God, his sisters and brothers and mothers, who were therefore also sisters and brothers and mothers to each other.[11]

Within the self-referential academic culture to which Bauckham belongs, and to which he constantly refers (around 450 references to modern authors in the book, 284 in this chapter alone), this probably cuts the mustard. But the voice of the real Junia/s (if ever it could be recalled with clarity) is being drowned out by the grinding of axes.

And what of poor Andronicus, the general reader will ask? Surely he was a "distinguished apostle," too, who deserves to be remembered and celebrated? Where is his extended biography? Who is there to sing his praises, or conjure him back from the shades? It seems somewhat unkind of Bauckham to treat him with such indifference—when his only crime is being neither a woman nor an interesting textual variant.

11. Ibid., 196.

Plate I: Peter Paul Rubens. Detail from *The Deposition*, 1602. Galleria Borghese, Rome.

Plate II: Matthias Grunewald. Detail from *The Isenheim Altarpiece*,
Musee Unterlinden, Colmar.

Plate III: Catacomb of Priscilla, Via Salaria, Rome. 'Fractio Panis'.

Plate IV: Catacomb of St Callixtus, Via Appia, Rome.

Plate V: Basilica of S. Pressede, Rome, Chapel of S.Zeno. The Lady Theodora alongside the patrons of the basilica and the Mother of God.

Plate VI: Detail of the above.

Plate VII: Basilica of S. Pressede, Rome, Apse. Pope Paschal I with S.Pressede and S. Peter.

Plate VIII: Interior of Siena Cathedral, showing the frieze of papal heads.

Plate IX: A 19th century Victorian Pope Joan board of unusual shape.

Plate X: Detail of the so-called Fractio Panis in the Catacomb of Priscilla,
Via Salaria, Rome.

Plate XI: Pope Joan publicly giving birth during a street procession. Note the jester behind the column mocking the event, as well as the Corinthian column which has the peculiar face of a demon. Woodcut engraving by Giovanni Boccaccio. Now in the British Museum. circa 1353.

5: Magdalena Apostola?

Often, if you want to write about women in history . . . you have to pretend that individual women were more important than they were, or that we know more about them than we do.

—HILARY MANTEL

"We know very little about Mary Magdalen." So Susan Haskins begins her book, *Mary Magdalen: Myth and Metaphor.*[1] Despite that frank admission, the modern bibliography of "Magdalen Studies" is extensive: Helen Garth, Victor Saxer, Marjorie Malvern, Katherine Jansen; the list goes on. Down the ages, the woman about whom little is known has been accorded a rich and complex biography. In art she has been represented variously, from the frankly lascivious (Peter Paul Rubens) to the heart-rendingly tragic (Matthias Grünewald). The Magdalen, like the Beloved Disciple—elusive and mysterious, part person and part symbol—has generated a devotion in the affective piety of Christians which cannot be ignored. But Haskins is undoubtedly right: we *know* very little. Professor E. P. Sanders in his magisterial *The Historical Figure of Jesus* puts the matter succinctly:

> Mary Magdalen has appealed enormously to people who have imagined all sorts of romantic things about her: she has been a prostitute, she was beautiful, she was in love with Jesus, she fled to France carrying his child. For all we know, on the basis of our sources, she was eighty-six, childless, and keen to mother unkempt young men.[2]

1. Haskins, *Mary Magdalen: Myth and Metaphor.*
2. Sanders, *Historical Figure of Jesus,* 74–75.

Paucity of information notwithstanding, the Magdalen has most recently become a feminist icon. No less a figure than Bishop Tom Wright has put himself forward as a Magdalenite; one who believes, on the precedent of the "apostola Apostolorum," that women should be bishops. The appearance in the garden to Mary, he thinks, requires a "radical re-evaluation of the role of women." In the Pauline list of resurrection appearances the women, he thinks, have been "air-brushed out of the account." "Apostolic ministry grows out of the testimony that Jesus is alive," he says, and that testimony we receive first from the women and in particular the Magdalen. They, then, are the first Apostles. "I cannot understand why that should be problematic if you are a biblical Christian." When such statements can be made by a scholar with an international reputation, it is time to look again at what the Bible says about this shadowy figure, and at what we can conclude from it.

The first, though rather negative, witness is Paul, whose testimony, written some forty or fifty years before John's account of the meeting in the garden, is summarily dismissed by Wright. In a list of various resurrection appearances (which do not include women) (1 Cor 15:5), Paul is quite clear that the first to see the Risen Lord was Peter (cf. Luke 24:34). Paul also, interestingly, includes an appearance to "the Twelve." In Mark's gospel (now usually thought to be the earliest), Mary of Magdala is first mentioned by name at Mark 15:40 where, together with Mary the mother of James and Joses, and Salome, she is singled out from a wider group of women who watch the crucifixion from some distance. The same trio go to the tomb (with spices for the anointing of the body); they find the stone rolled away and are addressed by a young man dressed in white who gives them a clear charge to inform the disciples *and Peter* (i.e., the apostolic college with its appointed head) that the risen Lord will meet them in Galilee. But the women are disobedient: they depart in fear and tell no one.

Matthew clings closely to Mark. "In reality," says Bultmann, "there is but one story." Mary Magdalene and "the other Mary," (probably "Mary the mother of James and Joses" at Matt 27:56) come to the tomb without spices. They receive the same message as in Mark, this time from "the angel of the Lord." On their way joyfully to inform the disciples, they encounter Jesus himself, who gives them a similar instruction for the disciples. They worship the risen Lord and clasp his feet (cf. the *noli me tangere* of John). These same women presumably give a message from Jesus to the eleven, who go to meet him in Galilee at a pre-ordained rendezvous.

It is Luke who mentions Mary of Magdala earliest in his narrative. She is one of a group of women who have been healed by Jesus and who provide for him (and the disciples?) from their private resources (Luke 8:2–3). Luke gives us brief details of two of them: Mary, "from whom seven devils had been driven out," and Joanna, "the wife of Herod's steward, Chuza." In Luke, an unspecified group of women go to the tomb to anoint the body. They find the stone rolled away and the tomb empty. They see two men in shining garments, who say that Jesus has risen and remind them of his prophecies about rising from the dead (cf. Luke 24:27). Mary Magdalen, Joanna, and Mary the mother of James are then named as among a group of women who tell the apostles of the apparition and the empty tomb. The disciples are incredulous; but, in some manuscripts, Peter (less so, perhaps, than the rest?) goes to the tomb and verifies the testimony of the women. According to Luke, the first disciples actually to *see* the Risen Lord are Cleopas and his companion on the Emmaus road (or Peter [Luke 24:34], if the appearance to him preceded theirs).

John's is the fullest account; but it is difficult to reconcile it with the Synoptics. In John 20, it is Mary of Magdala alone who comes to the tomb in the dawn darkness of the first day of the week. She finds the tomb empty, and runs to tell Peter and the Beloved Disciple. She does not tell them that the Lord is risen—a fact of which, at that point, she remains ignorant. She tells them rather: "They have taken the Lord away from the tomb and we do not know where they have laid him." Small wonder that the emerging *Magdalenamythos* conveniently ignores this detail. Who, after all, wants a proto-feminist heroine whose principal role is to invite in the men? Peter and the Beloved Disciple run to the tomb. The first to see the displaced grave clothes is the Beloved Disciple; but the first to enter is Peter. The first testimony to resurrection faith is that of the Beloved Disciple. "He saw and he believed." What did he see, and why did he believe, the intelligent reader is required to ask. The encounter of Mary with her risen Lord, beautiful and compelling as it is, with its solemn charge to tell the brethren that "I ascend to my Father . . ." is subsequent to the revelation of the resurrection to Peter and the Beloved Disciple. That presumably is why it is a declaration by the Lord about his impending glorification, not about his rising from the dead.

Modern feminist legend ignores most of these facts. Paradoxically, the feminist version is based on the long ending of Mark (16:9ff.), which most modern scholars agree to be a later addition. It goes like this:

When, during the Passion, the Twelve and the other male disciples deserted Jesus, the women, including Mary, stood loyally by him. It was to Mary that Jesus first showed himself after the Resurrection. She took the resurrection message to the cowardly men, who at first refused to believe her *because she was female*. But you can't keep a good woman down. The criteria set out in Acts 1:21 for a valid apostleship make it clear that the Magdalene was a true apostle (more than that, she was "apostola Apostolorum," the first of the Apostles). So the Church should admit women to Holy Orders.

Almost none of this is sustainable. In the Synoptics, Mary is not alone at the tomb, and in only one of them (Luke) is it explicit that the three women are messengers of the Resurrection to the rest of the disciples. Even there they are bidden by men in dazzling apparel, not commissioned by Jesus himself. It is true that Luke indicates incredulity on the part of those who have not yet seen the evidence; but some manuscripts (borrowing, perhaps, from Paul or John) mitigate this by the eagerness of Peter to go to the tomb and see for himself. There is, in any case, no suggestion that the other disciples (why are they assumed to be exclusively male?) disbelieved the women *because they were women*, but rather, as the text makes clear, because their story seemed intrinsically incredible. Matthew, it is true, records a commissioning of the women by Jesus himself. But context establishes beyond question that, by comparison with the Great Commission at Matt 28:19, theirs is a limited task. The women are sent to the apostles ("my brethren"). It is the brethren ("the eleven"), by contrast, who are sent to all the world. Mary, of course, is famously the lone figure at the tomb in John's account; but John does not make her the messenger of the Resurrection to the Twelve. The message she gives to Peter and "the other disciple," is her own surmise from the disturbance of the stone; it is conjecture, not kerygma. The Risen Lord later gives her instructions to tell "my brethren" about his forthcoming ascension—but not the resurrection or the empty tomb, about which by this time they already know.

One aspect of John's account of the meeting between Jesus and Mary remains puzzling—and has interested commentators far less than one might have expected. Mary is forbidden to touch the Lord's risen body— the famous *Noli me tangere* which is the subject of so many Renaissance paintings. (This is in marked contrast with Matthew, where the women "clasped Jesus's feet.") A good deal of ingenuity has been expended in order to explain this strange command. Was John suggesting that the risen Christ was somehow intangible, like Homer's wraiths? Or did the command, as Teresa Okure[3] has suggested, form part of a commissioning of Mary by Jesus, a kind of apostolic "sending?" "John may be saying both that Jesus was indeed graspable, and that Mary was to go and get on with her new task," says Tom Wright.[4] But such attempts are in danger of missing the point. A week later Thomas is given an opposite command. "Give me your hand; put it into my side. Doubt no longer but believe." One thinks of the rendering by Carravaggio, in which few things could be more carnal than that probing finger. The question has to be: why the conflicting instructions?

There is, I think, an explanation—one which makes sense in terms of the overall patterning of the ending of John's Gospel (supposing, with most commentators, that chapter 21 is a later addition by another hand). "Happy are those who have not seen and yet believe" are the last words spoken by Jesus in John's account. And it is to those who have not seen—a new generation of Christians—that the evangelist dedicates his book: "These [things] are recorded so that you may believe . . . and that believing you may have life through his name." This most "spiritual" gospel, then, ends with a short treatise on the relationship between faith and evidence. The reader is taken through the evidence of the five senses: *sight, hearing, touch, smell,* and *taste.* They are, the evangelist is teaching us, *conducive* to faith but, even taken together, they do not constitute faith itself. The final sense, *taste,* is the most elusive—and yet proves the most persuasive.

The key to the story of the risen Jesus is the account of the resuscitation of Lazarus. The reader is expected to remember the details of the earlier story in order to unravel the mystery of the second. So it will be as well to go through the relevant details. Lazarus has been dead for four days when Jesus arrives. Jesus himself ensures that this will be the case by an otherwise inexplicable delay. Jesus commands that the stone closing the tomb be rolled away. Mary objects because the corpse, by now, will be reeking. Lazarus comes out of the tomb at Jesus's command. He is still bound in his grave clothes, with a cloth over his head. Jesus instructs that he be unbound. In John's account of the resurrection of Jesus all these details are picked up, leading in some cases to apprehension and in others to misapprehension. Mary Magdalen comes to the tomb, and because the stone has already been rolled away she quite wrongly assumes that body snatchers have been at work: *misapprehension.* She calls Peter and "the other disciple."

3. Okure, "Significance Today of Jesus' Commission."

4. Wright, *Resurrection of the Son of God,* 666.

"The other disciple," who is first to the tomb but second to enter, "saw and believed": *apprehension*. The visual evidence was the disposition of the grave clothes (cf. John 11:44); the belief was in the resurrection (cf. John 20:31). So he (and perhaps Peter? [cf. Luke 24:35; 1 Cor 15:3–8]) is the first witness. These two say nothing of what they have concluded to Mary, who persists in her theory that the body has been stolen or moved. Even when she "sees" Jesus she mistakes him for someone else: *misapprehension*. Only his voice confirms his identity (cf. John 10:3–5). The Good Shepherd calls his sheep by her name, "Mary": *apprehension*. That very evening Jesus appears to "the disciples." Thomas refuses to believe until he has touched the risen body: *disbelief*. Eight days later (that is on the next "Lord's Day"), Jesus encourages him to do just that. "My Lord and my God": *belief*.

By this stage we have had the evidence of three senses. "The other disciple" (and perhaps Peter?) *saw*; Mary *heard*; Thomas *touched*. Smell and taste remain. *Smell* is the dog which did not bark in the night. There is no *smell*, though we know that there should be (cf. John 11:40, where the evangelist deliberately draws it to our attention). *Taste*, is the evidence presented to John's readers (who "have not seen and yet believe") on every first day of the week (the Lord's Day), when they gather to celebrate the resurrection. "My flesh is real food; my blood is real drink" (John 6:55); "I am the bread of life . . . if you do not eat the flesh of the Son of Man and drink his blood, you will not have life in you" (John 6:35, 6:53). In this way the evangelist teases out the relationship between faith and experience, between belief and perception. The author of the First Epistle of St. John obligingly recapitulates the program for us, in case we have missed it:

> Something which has existed from the beginning, that we have heard and we have seen with our own eyes, that we have watched and touched with our hands: the Word who is life—that is our subject . . . What we have seen and heard we are telling you so that you too may be in union with us as we are in union with the Father and with his Son Jesus Christ. We are writing this to you to make our own joy complete.[5]

And in precisely the Eucharistic context which John assumes of his readers, Thomas Aquinas mediates on these very themes from the end of John's Gospel in the *Adoro te*:

> Seeing, touching, tasting are in thee deceived:

5. 1 John 1:1–4.

How says trusty hearing? that shall be believed;
What God's Son has told me, take for truth I do;
Truth himself speaks truly or there's nothing true.[6]

Aquinas goes on, you will remember, in what is surely an oblique and poignant reference to himself, to cite doubting Thomas and the events in the room on that first Low Sunday.

If this reading of the end of the gospel is right, it changes perceptions of both the role and status of Mary Magdalen. No longer can it be claimed, on John's authority, that she has an absolute primacy. Instead she fits into the pattern of a typical Johannine riddle, in which primacy goes to "the other disciple," or possibly (in agreement with Paul and Luke) to Peter or, on further reflection, to the readers themselves—the blessed "who have not seen and yet believe."

It may help to place Mary of Magdala in a wider context if the accounts of the resurrection appearances in the whole of the New Testament are summarized in table form:

Matthew	Mark	Luke	John	Paul
Jerusalem		*Jerusalem and nearby*	*Jerusalem*	*No location (various?)*
Two Marys			Mary Magdalene	Cephas = Peter
		Two Disciples	"The disciples"	"The Twelve"
		Peter	"The disciples" *(one week later)*	500
				James
In Galilee		The Eleven		All the Apostles
The Eleven		and others		Paul

Viewing the resurrection appearances thus, as three of the evangelists and Paul recount them, gives a clear idea of the status of the Magdalen within the actual scriptural evidence. What emerges is a confused picture which makes it hard to see how Bishop Tom Wright could arrive at his bullish confidence in the primacy of Mary and its significance for today's church. There is an obvious problem which relates to all the recorded appearances: they cannot all be right. So which is to be preferred? An assessment needs to be made, and obviously the criteria for that assessment cannot and

6. Eucharistic Hymn of St. Thomas Aquinas, translated by G. M. Hopkins.

should not involve prior conclusions about life in the modern church. Nor can any of the accounts be dismissed as part of a "male conspiracy," since all were written by men.

It seems sensible to begin with the list in 1 Corinthians 15, both because it was written first, and because it has a number of suggestive elements. The evangelists, of course, are writing narrative: they are telling a story. Stories require named characters about whom (preferably) something is already known. That is how a storyteller earns credibility. Their accounts vary in dramatic intensity, culminating with John's. Paul, on the other hand, did not need to take notice of any of those requirements. He had no need of narrative verisimilitude because he is simply giving us a list. It is one on which he himself appears. "And last of all he appeared to me too." Paul's witness and ministry gain credibility from the fact that he can give a testimony like that of the others. (That is why Paul insists that what he saw was "a spiritual body"; he could have said simply "a spirit"). It is because Paul's own claim to apostolic status depends upon his place on the list that we can be sure that he is giving us as accurate an account as he is able. Paul could not assume that he was the only source of information available to the Corinthians, nor can we. In any case, the Lord who had appeared to everyone on the list was soon to return. All would then be revealed; light would be cast on the veracity of Paul's account.

The question, however, remains: why are there no women on Paul's list, when all four gospels record women at the tomb? Like so many other questions about the scanty female involvement in the gospels, this is often presented as a loaded question expecting a feminist answer. But it is not the only question. As well ask why there are women in the other accounts, in a period when the testimony of women was so ill regarded. As well ask why in Mark's account there is no resurrection appearance at all, and why the disobedient women (Mary Magdalen among them) "said nothing to a soul." The presence of women at the crucifixion and at the tomb is easily explicable in terms of narrative credibility. Keening the fate of those undergoing capital punishment, and preparing bodies for burial, was women's work. They would be there, wouldn't they? The absence of the male disciples from Calvary is equally explicable: male accomplices of a man accused of sedition would be wise to keep their distance: prudence, not cowardice. But the rest of the questions—why different women? why different outcomes? why different details?—are in the end a matter not of historical research, but of literary criticism. I have tried to show how the patterning of ideas about faith and evidence shapes the conclusion of John's gospel, and how that affects the status and significance of Mary Magdalen. Similar literary judgements need to be made about the narrative purpose of the other three authors. Austin Farrer famously opined that the choice between the short and long endings of Mark's gospel was, in the end, a matter of literary taste. Something like that is probably the case with regard to the other writers' accounts. But that is a topic beyond the scope of this book.

Despite all these facts, the title "apostola Apostolorum" (apostle to the Apostles), which seems to have first gained general currency among the mendicant orders in the late twelfth century, has persisted. It has recently become the rallying cry of those in favor of women bishops. Two questions naturally arise: what, in New Testament terms, is meant by an "apostle"— what, as they say, is the job description? And what, applied to Mary Magdalen, might the title have meant to those who first used it?

Rather surprisingly, "apostle" begins its life as a nautical term. Originally the name of a sort of transport ship, it later came to refer to the dispatch of a fleet. Before the first century, only Herodotus is recorded using the word in the sense of "messenger." Josephus uses it to refer to an embassy sent to Rome—though that, of course, would have involved a journey by sea. Various theories have been floated about the origin of the word in relation to Rabbinic Hebrew, the most suggestive being as a translation of *sheliach* ("a plenipotentiary representative"). But New Testament usage seems much looser than that: Epaphroditus (Phil 2:25) is less a plenipotentiary and more a courier. The common denominator of the various theories seems to be that the word had come to mean simply "someone dispatched or sent on behalf of another." "Apostolos" occurs seventy-nine times in the New Testament: once in Mark, once in Matthew, once in John, six times in Luke, twenty-eight times in Acts, and twenty-seven times in the Pauline epistles. The key passage in Acts is, of course, the choice of Matthias to replace Judas. Gunter Klein in his book *The Twelve Apostles* describes this as the "Magna Carta," which established the concept of "the Twelve."[7]

> We must therefore choose someone who has been with us the whole time that the Lord Jesus was travelling around with us, someone who was with us right from the time when John was baptising until the day when he was taken up from us—and can act with us as a witness to his resurrection.[8]

7. Klein, *Twelve Apostles*, 197.

8. Acts 1:21–22.

It has rightly been remarked that, as a job description, this is strangely limiting. The requirements are not only stringent (ruling out many to whom the term "apostle," in its more general sense, might apply), but also temporally limited. There would inevitably come a time when no one living could fulfill the requirements. It was a job, moreover, for which there were unlikely to be many vacancies. The original Twelve were relatively young men. Whatever Luke's views about the coming parousia, those whose decision he recorded in Acts obviously expected it imminently: they were not laying the foundations of a new institution, but keeping alive one of the signs of the End. At the time of the election of Matthias, one person who would have been eminently qualified (from what we are told about her in the gospels) would indeed have been Mary Magdalen. According to Luke she had been around from the early days in Galilee, perhaps from the time of John's baptism, and according to Matthew and John she had seen the risen Lord. The reason that her name was not on the list is not because of some misogynistic conspiracy by Peter and the rest, but stems from that very temporal limitation. The time limit makes clear what the purpose of the election was: to perpetuate a sign which Jesus himself had given. "The Twelve" were the twelve sons of Jacob/Israel redivivus, a sign that the tribes were being gathered in (Mic 2:12; Isa 11:11f.), the nations being called to the temple of the Lord of Hosts (Isa 56:6–8; Zech 2:11), and that the kingdom was "nearer now than when we first believed" (Rom 13:11). For all these reasons the Twelve were symbolically and necessarily men. To have chosen a woman to replace Judas would have been to subvert the Lord's original intention—a change so fundamental as to be unthinkable.

Acts refers to Paul as an apostle only twice—and then in the plural, in conjunction with Barnabas. Paul, of course refers to himself as an apostle repeatedly. His claim (1 Cor 15:3–10) is based upon a resurrection appearance of Jesus and a special commission from him. Paul was clearly aware of the symbolic significance of "the Twelve" (so much so that he records a resurrection appearance to them when they could only have been eleven!). He does not claim to be one of their number, but by virtue of his calling and his having seen the risen Lord, their equal. A difficulty for Paul, and perhaps the reason for Luke's looser use of the term in referring to him, is another time limit on apostleship which Acts implies. Resurrection appearances, according to Luke, took place only within a period of forty days (Acts 1:3). Elaine Pagels, always sensitive to the smell of rodent, sees this as a later and illegitimate, institutional limitation on the exercise of charismatic ministry:

"the question revolves around whether direct access to Christ is available by means of special revelations 'through visions long after the resurrection' and whether such revelations are granted to certain persons and not to others."[9] Paul, sensitive to the problems created by unruly visionaries in Corinth, probably saw the point, but stuck to his guns.

Conspiracy theories, of course, are rife among Christian feminists, but there seems to be no reason to think that a conscious (or even unconscious) process of exclusion was at work in the use of the term "apostle." More likely two uses ran concurrently—one, as applied to Barnabas and Epaphroditus, varied between "messenger" and "special messenger"; the other applied only to the Twelve, who were chosen by Jesus and named as such (Luke 6:13). Both usages have stuck. Most people hearing the word "apostle" think instinctively of the Twelve. But the looser application is also common, and the two are never confused. Usage can indeed be very loose. Gregory the Great, for example, who never set foot in the country, is sometimes called "the Apostle of the English." It is this double sense which enables the play on words involved in the title "apostola Apostolorum." Feminists, of course stress temporal priority: Mary gets the message first and passes it on to the other disciples, who are in that sense secondary. We have seen that the temporal priority of the women is dubious, to say the least. But in any case, that is not the only, or even I suggest the most natural interpretation of the texts. The women's task was limited; they were given a specific charge directed only to the disciples. "Go and tell my brothers that they must leave for Galilee . . ." (Matt 28:10). "Go and find the brothers, and tell them that I am ascending . . ." (John 20:17). The task of the Apostles, on the contrary, is universal. It is to the "eleven" on the Galilean mountain that the Great Commission is given. "Go, therefore, make disciples of all the nations . . ." (Matt 28:19). The clue is in the use of *adelphoi* (brothers), which occurs in both relevant gospels. Inglorious as the role may seem to those who are looking for more, the women in both these gospels have a specific message to relay to particular people. They are apostles to the Apostles: messengers to the Twelve.

* * *

It may seem strange, in view of all this, that a seasoned scholar of otherwise unimpeachable reputation like Tom Wright should accept as gospel the current myth of the Magdalen and belatedly scramble onto the feminist

9. Pagels, "Visions, Appearances," 424.

bandwagon. But it is worth reflecting that, though the Magdalen provides no conceivable precedent for women's ordination, the sort of fantasies that have arisen around her are not uncommon. If a character—fictional or historical—is engaging, or merely mysterious, we want to know more. The apocryphal gospels are full of material designed to "fill in" perceived gaps or satisfy idle curiosity. Shakespeare, legend has it, was under pressure to reprise his greatest creation, Sir John Falstaff. The object lesson is that even he managed only the sad travesty of *The Merry Wives of Windsor*. In a bold proto-feminist moment Mary Cowden Clarke—author of the invaluable *Concordance to Shakespeare*—produced *The Girlhood of Shakespeare's Heroines*,[10] succumbing to the seductive notion that because they were persuasive as characters in a play, these women could be treated as though they were real people, with histories independent of the pieces in which they had originally appeared.

No character in fiction, however, has excited as much interest as the fleeting appearances in the gospels of Mary Magdalen. The development begins, no doubt, with her star turn in the garden. It is easy to see how fertile imaginations could feed on those sparse details. "*Mary!*" Was it perhaps a nickname, a pet name, a sign of intimacy, allowing the Magdalen, through her tears, to see her beloved more clearly? "*Do not touch me!*" There surely was proof of past intimacies now tragically withdrawn! In a leap and a bound the imagination is all the way to Tim Rice and Andrew Lloyd-Webber:

> What's it all about? Yet, if he said he loved me, I'd be lost. I'd be frightened. I couldn't cope, just couldn't cope. I'd turn my head. I'd back away. I wouldn't want to know. He scares me so. I want him so. I love him so.[11]

Though this version of the Magdalen fits seamlessly into the milieu of the modern West End musical, sentimentality has not always been Mary's strong suit. Her life after death began in the struggle between orthodoxy and Gnosticism in the first and second centuries of the Christian era.

We once knew little about this period. A few surviving documents, along with the condemnations of vehement opponents of heresy like Epiphanius of Salamis (c.315–403), were all that testified to the faith of Gnostic Christians. Then in 1945, in the sands of Upper Egypt, a library

---

10. Clarke, *Girlhood of Shakespeare's Heroines*.
11. Webber (music) and Rice (lyrics), *Jesus Christ Superstar*.

was discovered (52 documents in all) which aroused widespread interest. Unlike the Dead Sea Scrolls, which were found in Palestine two years later, the Nag Hammadi collection quickly became available to the general public.[12] The best-known text from this treasure trove was the Gospel of Thomas, first translated into English in 1959. Interest intensified in the late 1970s when all the remaining documents appeared in translation. In 1979, Elaine Pagels, the doyenne of Gnostic studies, produced her masterpiece of popularization, "The Gnostic Gospels." The 1970s and 1980s, of course, were a heady era for feminists. Mary Daly's "The Church and the Second Sex" had appeared in 1968, Rosemary Radford Reuther's "New Woman, New Earth" in 1975, Elisabeth Schussler Fiorenza's "In Memory of Her" in 1983. The translation of the Nag Hammadi library had fortuitously coincided with an explosion of feminist theology (Karen Armstrong, "The Gospel according to Woman," 1987; Rosemary Radford Reuther, "Gaia and God," 1992; Ursula King, "Women and Spirituality," 1993), at the center of which would now be the figure of the Magdalen, seen through the distorting lens of Gnostic speculation. The recently recovered past seemed to be speaking to the present in a way little short of uncanny. "The Nag Hammadi source," wrote Elaine Pagels, "discovered in a time of contemporary social crises concerning sexual roles, challenges us to reinterpret history—and to re-evaluate the present situation."[13]

As a matter of fact, the myth which was being spun by feminist commentators on the new Gnostic texts was by no means original. It was a reworking of the age-old myth of the Fall. In the beginning was "The Jesus Movement": spontaneous, unstructured, counter cultural, charismatic, egalitarian. The history of the earliest Christian communities, it was being claimed, was the history of a Fall into Patriarchy; in consequence of which, by the end of the second century, the Church had become hierarchical, dogmatic, and androcentric. From the Gnostic texts emerged the notion of a power struggle between the female prophets, presbyters, bishops, and apostles (who were held to have proliferated in the primitive period), and the apostolic succession of male hierarchs which relentlessly sought to displace them. In the Pistis Sophia, (discovered 1773, and probably dating from the second century) the antagonism is personalized. Mary Magdalen is commended by Jesus for possessing, through the divine *gnosis*, a deeper knowledge and wisdom than the male apostles. Peter remonstrates with Jesus: "My Lord, we are not able

12. Robinson, J. M., *Nag Hammadi Library in English.*
13. Blurb for the 1988 edition of *The Nag Hammadi Library in English.*

to suffer this woman . . ." Mary rejoins: "I am afraid of Peter, for he threatens me and he hates our race [i.e., sex]." Miriam Winter, in a fictional "Gospel according to Mary," 1970 (not to be confused with the gnostic text of the same name), writes in a manner reminiscent of *1984*:

> There was even talk of a canon, of making certain traditions authoritative for all. Women everywhere were disheartened. Their leadership was no longer recognised. Their experience was being misinterpreted. Their preaching, teaching and prophesying had been disqualified on theoretical grounds . . . Was it the end of the age of freedom? Would wisdom disappear in the heat of theological definition? Soon no one would remember how it had once been.[14]

This myth of a golden age lost or destroyed is the recurrent theme of many movements. The Reformation of the sixteenth century saw itself as restoring a primitive Christianity that had been corrupted by the accretions of time and the rapacity of the Roman Church. The Renaissance looked through the "Dark Ages" to the refulgence of the classical past. All such myths have a problem with evidence. They envisage the past as they want the present to be; and their imagination is more powerful than their historical sense. Most of the gnostic documents which have been used to uncover the earliest "Christianities," and finesse the canonical gospels, are late in date and suspect in style and content. If the critical techniques applied to the New Testament by the Questers for the historical Jesus were applied to them, very little would remain. But they have, of course, been treated with a generosity that is denied to the official canon.

The Mary Magdalen who emerges from this doubtful reconstruction is the female leader of an egalitarian movement; in some versions a rival of Jesus, certainly a rival of Peter and the Twelve. She symbolizes the nameless women who are thought to have stood against the rising tide of authoritarianism and centralization brought about by the new male hierarchy, symbolized by the jealous male apostles. That there was intense conflict in the second and third centuries between the orthodox and various heretical movements (Valentinians, Montanists, Ophites, Marcellians, etc.) is beyond doubt. We now have documents detailing the gnostic side of the story—a useful corrective to the picture painted by the orthodox controversialists whose writings had come down to us. But in this literary slanging match, it makes sense to view the claims of both sides with equal suspicion. To seek to find their

---

14. Winter, *Gospel According to Mary*, 91.

conflicts and concerns in the New Testament—in documents written two centuries before, in a very different world—makes no sense at all.

If we turn from 1970s speculations about second century Gnosticism to the Magdalen of the patristic period, we find someone quite different. Here we are presented with six characters in search of an author. The Fathers, particularly in the East, were exercised in finding a typology for this enigmatic female saint. In a Commentary on the Song of Songs (once attributed to Hippolytus, bishop and martyr of Rome d. 253) Mary and Martha (sic) go together to the tomb, meet Jesus and are the first witnesses to his resurrection. From the pairing with Martha of Bethany we can probably assume that this is Mary Magdalen. Probably to counter their incredulity as reported in the long ending of Mark, the disciples receive a special visit from Jesus to assure them of the veracity of the sisters: "It is I who appeared to these women, and I who wanted to send them to you as apostles." So begins what Marina Warner has described as "the muddle of Marys." Ambrose (possibly following Eusebius) joins the fray with the suggestion that there might have been two Magdalens. In a discourse sometimes attributed to Cyril of Jerusalem, Mary the Mother of Jesus is added to the confusion, when the author claims that the Virgin herself had spoken to him: "I am Mary Magdalen because the name of the village where I was born was Magdala. My name is Mary of Cleopas. I am Mary of James the son of Joseph the carpenter." A similar conflation/confusion appears in a Coptic text ascribed to the Apostle Bartholemew, where Jesus appears after the resurrection to his mother. She greets him with Mary Magdalen's "rabbouni," and is then commissioned to take the news of his rising to the disciples. Mary asks: "Jesus my Lord and my only Son, bless me . . . if only you will allow me to touch you." All this is a development which M. R. James scathingly described as "the reckless identification of the Virgin Mary with all the other Maries of the gospels."

Moving in an opposite direction, typology which was later and more appropriately applied to the Virgin seems to have begun life associated with the Magdalen. She was seen, by virtue of the message she supposedly brought to the other disciples, as a second Eve. Referring to Mary Magdalen, Augustine himself proclaimed: "per feminem mors, per feminem vita"; and Hilary of Poitiers preached the same. Who knows where the speculation might have ended: Mary Magdalen as co-redemptrix? But another development cut short the process. Gregory the Great, in a sermon preached in San Clemente in Rome in 591, severed the tangle of Marys, by creating the character who was to dominate the Middle Ages: he identified Mary with Luke's repentant sinner, and so brought the Magdalen too close to Eve for comfort. That sermon made possible—inevitable even—the whole subsequent development. It is to be doubted that this collapse of three distinct gospel identities into one—Mary of Bethany, with the sinner with the perfume, with Mary Magdalen—was original to Gregory. But he gave it the stamp of Papal authority which licensed everything which followed. Devotion to the Virgin now began to impinge on the status of the Magdalen. A lively tradition arose (ignoring the total absence of any such suggestion in the New Testament), affirming that Jesus's first resurrection appearance had been, not to Peter, nor to Mary Magdalen (the two protagonists in the earlier Gnostic conflict), but to his mother. The absence of scriptural warranty, however, proved too serious a problem. In any case, things were soon to take a quite different turn. Mary Magdalen had been re-invented; she was now to be relocated. It is at this stage that the story takes on at least some of the elements of a Dan Brown novel.

The great Romanesque basilica at Vezelay in the heart of Burgundy was originally dedicated to Our Lady. Around the middle of the eleventh century the property came under new management. And the new proprietor, Abbot Geoffrey, put it under the patronage of another Mary. In 1058, a papal bull recognized the abbey's claim to possess the relics of Mary Magdalen, and the new pilgrimage site (conveniently situated on one of the routes to the shrine of St. James at Compostella) was open for business. Like all antiquities, relics need a provenance. Fortunately, legend already had it that Mary and her companions, fleeing the persecution of Christians in the Holy Land, had been set adrift in a rudderless boat (think: Volto Santo of Lucca) which was washed up at Marseilles. The Magdalen, the story went, had set about the successful conversion of the heathen Gauls, then left her companion Maximin to become the first Bishop of Marseilles, and retired to a cave to live out her life in reclusive contemplation (think: St. Mary of Egypt, with whom the Magdalen seems to have been at different times confused or collated). She was buried at Saint-Maximin-en-Provence. It was from Saint Maximin that the monk Badilus was claimed to have stolen the remains from under the noses of invading Visigoths (think: St. Mark and Venice; the *translatio*), and taken them safely to Vezelay. (All this, it has to be said, was quite unremarkable in the eleventh century, which had seen the transfer to Western Europe of a number of other New Testament luminaries: St. James to Galicia, Dionysius the Areopagite to the Ile de France, and Joseph of Arimathaea to Glastonbury. For none of these translations is there a single scrap of evidence.)

The story, however, does not end there. A century or so later, Provence had its revenge. The Dominican author of the *Legenda Aurea*, Jacobus de Voragine (d. 1298), carefully chronicled the miracles of the Magdalen at Vezelay, in a work which become something of a medieval best-seller. The book came to the attention of Charles of Anjou, Count of Provence and soon to be King of Naples (he was also a generous supporter of the Order of Preachers). Charles, no doubt in search of a significant patron for his expanding empire in the south, became convinced that Mary Magdalen's body still rested at St. Maximin; and in 1279, he duly—and miraculously—discovered her (think: St. Mark in Venice again; the *inventio*). This invention was celebrated with great pomp, and the monastery of St. Maximin given into the care of the Dominican Order.

"Be careful what you write about the Magdalen," said a priest friend of mine who had got wind that I was writing this chapter. "The Dominicans are very fond of her." Mary had, indeed, gained not only a new home, but with it new and influential friends. They naturally identified with her closely, for they were themselves re-evangelizing the territory which legend had it that she had first Christianized. And paradoxically, in the Albigensian Crusade, they were combating heresies akin to the Gnosticism of the era in which she had originally risen to prominence. Basing themselves on eastern legends of Mary's preaching in Palestine, the Order of Preachers made a preacher out of the Magdalen, and a shining exception to the Pauline prohibition. Not to be outdone, the Franciscans, for their part, turned her into an exemplum of affective piety. The two mendicant orders had each adopted as their own an appropriate and characteristic element of the tradition: the Dominicans seized on the Magdalen who sat at Jesus's feet in the house at Bethany, and was pre-eminently a student of the word; the Franciscans meditated on the Mary who had washed Jesus's feet with her tears, and taking the hint from her presence on Calvary, imagined those tears being poured out at the very foot of the Cross.

By the end of the thirteenth century, Mary Magdalen—the woman about whom little is known—had become a character in her own right, almost free of her scriptural origins. It remained only, on the grounds of her identification with Luke's sinner, to make of her the perfect example of penance and remorse. Though Catholics continued to see her also as a mystic and a contemplative, for Protestants she became, almost exclusively, the penitent whore. Her name was a euphemism for "prostitute"; reformatories for fallen women were known as Magdalen Houses. And, in a final cruel twist, she became a dedicated follower of fashion: society ladies of the Age of Enlightenment rejoiced to be painted as Weeping Magdalens, for the titillation of their beaux.

None of this extravagant catalogue of improbabilities could have prepared one, however, for the resurrection of the Magdalen in the twentieth century as a feminist icon. Nothing, on the face of it, could be more improbable. Just as the principles of the Enlightenment were finally taking root among Christians (and belief in the miraculous—including the bodily Resurrection—was waning among Church-goers), Mary Magdalen embarked on a new career. On the strength of her close encounter in the garden, Mary became a principal argument for the ordination of women as bishops. But there is an obvious problem, which seems to have escaped the notice of over-enthusiastic commentators. A survey undertaken by Christian Research in 2002 showed that only 53% of female clergy of the Church of England (though 68% of male clergy) any longer believes that Jesus was bodily resurrected.[15] What, one is obliged to ask, does this substantial minority of women priests think happened in that Levantine garden so long ago? And why, whatever it was, do they think it should have any bearing on church order two millennia later, or their place in it?

This brief and hectic summary of the afterlife of the girl from Migdal shows without a shadow of doubt that she had become a woman for all seasons. Different ages, institutions and individuals reshaped her, and found themselves reflected in her. Her function, far removed from her fleeting appearance in the New Testament, has been to give each age back to itself. Never more so than in our own age and generation. The bibliography of "Magdalen Studies" since the late 1990s, is a publishing phenomenon in its own right. Much of it takes the form of a recapitulation of what Philip Jenkins has memorably called "fragments of a faith forgotten"; the attempt to rescue from oblivion faint traces of a fugitive world—one more congenial to the writers than the present. Bishop Tom Wright had got the measure of it back in 1998 when he wrote that this alternative history "appears to legitimate precisely the sort of religion that a large swathe of America yearns for: a free-for-all, do-it-yourself spirituality with a strong agenda of social protest . . . You can have any sort of spirituality you like . . . as long as it isn't orthodox Christianity."[16]

15. Brierley, *Mind of Anglicans.*

16. Wright, "Return to Christian Origins," 10.

6: Mosaics, Catacombs and Concelebrations

This art is an easy-going one, indifferent to detail, to the individual expression of the figure, to the precise traits of the face . . . these paintings of the catacombs are not meant to represents events—they only suggest them.

—ANDRE GABAR

The number 319 bus lumbers out of the bus station next to the Stazione Termini, negotiates the Largo Argentina, enters the faceless suburbs, and ends up on the Via Saleria opposite a nondescript nunnery, with a narrow entrance and a small modern chapel (nearest bus stop: Via di Priscilla). An elderly nun, chattering in Italian far too rapid for easy comprehension, will lead you through the gloomy galleries to what has become the most famous fresco in Rome. In the Cappella Graeca of the Catacomb of Priscilla is a painting of seven shadowy, indistinct figures seated together at a table. The condition of the fresco is poor. It will not be improved by the number of visitors it now attracts, bringing moisture and body heat into a confined space. Most visitors will have seen, or will see on leaving, the modern mosaic which clothes the wall behind the *versus populum* altar in the nuns' small chapel. It is a rather romanticised version of the fresco below, and must surely remind every visitor of the more famous fresco by Leonardo. The resemblance, alas, ends with the disposition of figures: they are seated behind a table and facing the spectator. That is all. It is no great work of art.

In a program [*Everyman: The Hidden Tradition*] broadcast on Sunday, November 8, 1992 (the Sunday before the final vote on the ordination of women in the General Synod of the Church of England), it was claimed that the fresco in the Cappella Graeca of the Catacomb of Priscilla and a mosaic in the Chapel of S. Zeno in the Church of S. Praxedis (both in Rome) are, respectively, representations of seven women concelebrating the eucharist and of a woman bishop, the mother of Pope Pascal I. Writing of the program in a book dedicated to its producer, Angela Tilby, her friend Lavinia Byrne speaks of the power of the visual evidence—a male celebrant—which has been persistently set before Christian congregations for time out of mind. "No wonder they think they know what a priest should look like!" Byrne adds: "Only in darkened catacombs, or, ambiguously, in mosaics, are there images which tell a different story."[1] Ambiguously, indeed! For, though those images surface as "evidence" in a number of unexpected places including a pamphlet by the veteran Scottish Presbyterian theologian T. F. Torrance,[2] all the references can be traced back to a single source—Joan Morris's slender volume of 1974.[3] (Morris, a venerable Catholic feminist who died in 1985, was—not entirely co-incidentally—the first modern popularizer of the story of her namesake, Pope Joan.) None of these references, however, (including their *fons et origo*) even attempts to give a serious academic account of the evidence. Torrance, for example, seems to think (as does Morris) that the Catacomb of Priscilla has some connection with the wife of Aquila (Acts 18:1–3, 18–19; Rom 16:3–5; 1 Cor 16:19; 2 Tim 4:19). Torrance even maintains that the fresco includes representations of Priscilla and her husband. Such is, of course, very far from probable. The catacomb dates from the end of the second century, and was excavated below a villa of the *gens Acilia*, fragments of which survive. It is not known when it received its present name, but a corruption of the original name of the property cannot be ruled out. The Capella Graeca is so-called on account of the Greek inscriptions over one of its niches, with dedications by a certain Obrinus (of whom nothing else is known) to his cousin and companion Palladius and to his wife, Nestoriana. The fresco is dated by most authorities to the late third century.

So what are these pictures, and why have they stirred such uncritical enthusiasm? The Capella Graeca painting is of seven figures seated ("intimately," says Byrne) at the opposite side of a table from the spectator. To either side, set on the ground, are six (or seven) containers, which appear

1. Byrne, *Woman at the Altar*, 50.

2. Torrance, *Ministry of Women*.

3. Morris, J., *Against Nature and God*.

to be either jars or baskets. Some may (or may not) contain bread. The condition of the fresco is poor, but it is certainly the case that at least one of the figures is female. The figure at the extreme left has arms extended and may (or may not) have a beard. Who are they, and what are they doing? Professor Torrance appears to be in no doubt:

> In one of the earliest (sic) catacomb paintings in Rome in the Capella Greca, within a century after the death and resurrection of Christ (sic), there is a remarkable mural depicting the breaking of bread at the celebration of the eucharist. Seven presbyters are seated in a semicircle behind the Holy Table, assisted by several deacons. This is known as the "Catacomb of Priscilla" for Priscilla is seated to the right of the presiding presbyter (presumably her husband, Aquila, the *proestos* or bishop), and is actively engaged with him in the eucharisitc rite.[4]

Torrance then goes on to a lengthy explanation of why there are seven figures. But his fanciful speculation need not detain us now, for a more important feature of his account demands our attention: ". . . assisted," says Torrance, "by several deacons." Deacons, of course, are exactly what one would expect at a eucharistic celebration of the proposed period. The liturgical textbooks are full of the role of the deacon in the Patristic liturgy. At the time I first read his paper I had, I confess, seen only a photograph of the fresco—a postcard sent me by a member of the committee of the Movement for the Ordination of Women (MOW). It showed no "deacons." Imagine, then, the excitement with which I mounted the bus for the lengthy journey up the Via Salaria, toward what would be my first viewing of the painting in its entirety. Alas! After a lengthy descent in the company of the obligatory talkative nun, no deacons! What you see—postcard-wise—is what you get. There are seven figures and no more. Quite simply, Torrance was making these extraordinary and specific claims about a painting he had never actually seen!

Mary Ann Rossi (as interviewed for Angela Tilby's award-winning television program) saw something else.

> It was most striking to me to realise that these were seven women sitting around the table. And it really strikes you when you see something you had not expected, and suddenly it is brought home. There is no doubt; I think you will agree when you have seen it, that they are seven women and not seven men . . . If you look at

4. Torrance, "Ministry of Women: An Argument."

the shape of the people, these are not men. Women are not built the same! The presence, the aspect, the gestures! Ah, they seem to be self-assured, happy in their celebration. It's a look I have seen on the faces of women with whom I have been celebrating Mass in my country. It's a satisfaction, it's a happiness, it's a self-assured posture that I see in the seven women in the Priscilla painting.[5]

Rossi's effusive account is, sadly, incompatible with Torrance's equally categorical assertion. Clearly the picture cannot, at one and the same time, represent seven concelebrating women, and a mixed company (with deacons!) in which a man (Aquila) and his wife (Priscilla) are concelebrating. In her television program, Canon Tilby (as she now is) wisely kept Rossi and Torrance apart. They follow one another, but they never meet. One cannot help thinking, however, what fun she missed by not taking the pair of them to Rome (at the expense of the BBC), standing them together in front of the fresco, and letting them battle it out. The program might have been more honest—and entertaining—as a result. There are, of course, several problems which make both readings of the picture improbable. It is true that, almost since Joseph Wilpert's "discovery" of the fresco in the nineteenth century, it has been called the "*Fractio Panis*"; and that a copy of it, in mosaic, has been used by the nuns, who are now its custodians, as an altar piece in their convent chapel since the 1960s. It is also true that the composition—a number of figures facing the spectator from behind a table—irresistibly reminds anyone who sees it of the most famous of all representations of the Last Supper. But is this a picture of a eucharistic celebration? And if so, a celebration in what circumstances or context?

Torrance writes of a "presiding presbyter . . . the *proestos* or bishop," (whom he identifies as "presumably her husband Aquila") and of Priscilla (as he confidently claims) "actively engaged with him in the eucharistic rite." (Torrance, incidentally, was more definitive to camera than in the pamphlet.) Rossi speaks of "seven women concelebrating the eucharist," with the expressions of joy which she has seen in her own country when women were concelebrating the Mass. But what precisely, in either case, is envisaged? Torrance's slippery phrase ("actively engaged with him in the eucharistic rite"), acknowledges, I suspect, the existence of problems of which Rossi, in her sentimental reverie, is blissfully unaware. Concelebration in the strict sense of a college of priests reciting the anaphora together

5. In the television program by Tilby, *Everyman: The Hidden Tradition*, BBC broadcast Nov. 8, 1992.

is difficult to envisage at a time when the eucharistic prayer remained the extempore composition of the celebrant. "Christian texts of this type," says Bouyer (meaning written prayers of thanksgiving at the Eucharist), "become common only after the great crisis of Arianism, i.e., after the second half of the fourth century"[6]—which is to say: far beyond Torrance's incredible dating of the fresco to around 130 AD, and well beyond the generally agreed dating of around 290 AD. The first firm evidence of concelebration in the modern sense relates to Papal masses in the seventh century. Not until the twelfth century (as St. Thomas Aquinas attests) had it been exported from Rome and was common at ordinations elsewhere. It is sometimes suggested that, in the immediately sub-apostolic period, "concelebrating priests" stood beside their bishop raising their hands over the oblations in silence. But the evidence for such a practice is flimsy, and in any case it is not what is represented in the Capella Graeca. There the figures are clearly seated, and no common gesture defines them.

All this said, there must, I suppose, remain a question about Torrance's husband-and-wife team, who are both supposed to be "actively engaged" in a eucharistic rite. The question is: how would we know, from a painting, if this were the case? Necessarily, I suggest, by gesture. But by what gestures would the artist declare his intent? And are any such gestures apparent in this painting? And are all (or any) of the other participants engaged in them? To my eye there is no more evidence for Torrance's confidence in this matter than there is for the service of those "several deacons" whose absence from the fresco we have already noted. In an influential survey of paleo-Christian iconography, André Grabar comments:

> . . . in some cases the brevity [of the signs employed in catacomb paintings] is certainly excessive, as when, for example, a scene that represents a meal of some kind has no detail that would distinguish between the Multiplication of Loaves, the Miracle of Cana, the Last Supper or the repast in paradise beyond the tomb. Those who planned the mural paintings in the catacombs were probably not entirely averse to a certain ambiguity in their image-signs, since the Multiplication of the Loaves, for example, was regarded as a symbol of the agape of paradise or a figuration of the Last Supper.[7]

---

6. Bouyer, *Eucharist: Theology and Spirituality*, 136.

7. Grabar, *Christian Iconography: A Study*, 8–9.

This interpenetration of images, Grabar is emphasising, is precisely what catacomb art is all about. It is a style which eschews clarity and particularity. No observer, looking at the four scenes cited by Grabar could fail, however, to notice a significant feature of three of them. In three of the four, prominent in the composition (in front of the table in the Callixtus and Peter and Marcellinus frescoes [Grabar, plate 6, 9]; on either side of it in the Priscilla fresco [Grabar, plate 7]) there are a number of large containers. What are they, and what are they for? The challenge for those who believe that the paintings are representations of a eucharistic celebration is to give a plausible liturgical explanation of their use and purpose. And that, I suspect, cannot be done. The painting in the catacomb of SS. Peter and Marcellinus comes closest to giving us a clue. There, the seven figures at the table (seven again—it is always seven!) are joined by two more, one significantly larger than the other. The mysterious vessels are this time ranged out between these standing figures. The explanation generally given seems plausible enough. The large robed figure is Jesus, the smaller one the *architriklinos* (John 2:9), and the vessels are the six *hydriai* (John 2:6) whose contents are being turned into wine. The scene is the Wedding at Cana of Galilee: itself, of course, in John's gospel, a type of the eucharist. Are the vessels in the Callixtus and Priscilla frescoes water-pots in the same way? And is the "veiled woman" in the catacomb of "Priscilla" intended for the bride (another richly symbolic figure, in a richly symbolic story)? On the balance of evidence it seems highly probable; but we will never know for certain. Fabrizio Mancinelli, until recently Assistant Curator of Medieval, Modern, and Byzantine Art in the Vatican Museums, draws attention to another possibility. The fresco in the Catacomb of Callixtus, he points out, shows eleven containers (and here they seem clearly to be baskets) ranged on either side. Were there originally twelve (12 = *kophinoi* [Mark 6:43; John 6:13]; 7 = *kophinoi* [Mark 8:19]; 6 = *hydriai* [John 2:7])?

> The scene . . . could hardly be mistaken for a simple pagan funeral meal. It appears in several places in the Roman catacombs, and although it varies in form, it always contains the symbolic number of baskets filled with bread, a detail which is lacking in the frescoes which clearly depict a *refrigerium*, or funeral banquet. The baskets commemorate the miracle wrought by Jesus in the desert, when he provided bread for the famished multitude.[8]

8. Mancinelli, *Catacombs of Rome*, 24.

Mancinelli, moreover, sees a great deal more in the Priscilla painting than is apparent to others or to me:

> Sitting at the table are seven persons, among them a woman with veiled head. At the far left a bearded figure, dressed in tunic and pallium, extends his hands to break the bread (fractio panis). On the table before him are a chalice of wine, a plate with two fishes and one with five loaves of bread. The composition is bordered by seven baskets of bread, three to one side, four to the other.[9]

What I suggest is most illuminating about this story with no very firm conclusions, is not what we learn from it about the past, but what we learn about the present. Why, we need to ask, are intelligent people like Thomas Torrance and MaryAnn Rossi prepared to be so dogmatic about things about which they clearly know so very little? And why was Lavinia Byrne so ready to adopt a hermeneutic of suspicion with regard to Wilpert and his water-colorist? And why was Angela Tilby so eager to mislead viewers of her program about the scholarly consensus regarding a series of catacomb paintings which, whatever they are, are certainly not simple portrayals of a second century eucharist, by "concelebrants" either male or female? The answer is sad but obvious: they have leapt too enthusiastically from the ethical to the historical. That the Christian priesthood should be open equally to women as to men is for them a self-evident truth. And they have assumed that what ought to be, must have been. In disciplines like theology and church history, reliant as they are on pedigree and precedent, the temptation is obvious. But the practitioners are none the less culpable. Tom Torrance's "deacons" are a lesson to us all.

* * *

The church of S. Praxedis (Sta Prassede) stands close to the great Basilica of Sta Maria Maggiore. It was one of the Roman building projects of Pope Paschal I (pont. 817–24), who was buried there. In the chapel of St. Zeno, a small vaulted room off the main body of the basilica, is a mosaic representing Paschal's mother, the Lady Theodora, executed in her life-time (hence the square nimbus or halo). Again attention was drawn to the mosaic by Joan Morris in her book of 1972. Like the fresco in the Priscilla Catacomb, the reference was taken up by Tom Torrance:

---

9. Ibid., 29.

However, in spite of this depreciation of the female sex widely found in the Mediterranean Church, there were strange exceptions to the canonical restriction of clerical office to women. For instance, in a mosaic still extant in the Church of *Santa Praseda* in Rome, built by Pascal I toward the end of the ninth century in honour of four holy women, one of whom was his mother Theodora, we can still read around her head in bold letters *theodora episcopa*. And so we have papal authority for a woman bishop and an acknowledgement by the pope that he himself was the son of a woman bishop! The word *episcopa* was evidently used at times to refer to the wife of a bishop, as *presbytera* was sometimes used (and still is in Greece) to refer to the wife of a presbyter, but that does not seem to have been the case in this instance.[10]

I fear that the veteran Presbyterian was allowing his anti-papal sentiments to get the better of him. For there is no evidence whatever, apart from the inscription, that Theodora was a bishop, and ample testimony to the ancient practice of bestowing on the wife of a priest the courtesy title of *presbytera*. Here it is extended politely to the mother of a bishop. Dr Torrance did not need to cast his net as far as Greece for a modern parallel: many a Bavarian village has its Frau Doktor, who has no medical skills of her own! The simple fact is that Torrance has seized upon a text (*Theodora Episcopa)* without a context; and texts without context are easily misunderstood. To make his case Torrance would have needed to establish a credible environment in which the lady Theodora might have done her bishopping: a church in which her vocation might have been discerned, confirmed, and universally received. The truth surely is that, if such a church ever existed, the Roman Church of the ninth century was not it. A little context will help to explain why.

Paschal I is an interesting character. Prior of the convent of S. Stephano Rotondo on the Caelian Hill, he was unanimously elected Pope by his fellow presbyters, without reference to Louis the Pious, who had succeeded his father Charlemagne to the Empire. The omission caused tensions which were only resolved after several diplomatic missions from Rome to Aachen. Despite the rather off-hand response of the Council of Frankfurt (794) to Nicaea II (787), Paschal was an ardent opponent of iconoclasm, a supporter and correspondent of Theodore the Studite (759–826). He gave asylum in Rome to exiled monks fleeing the regime in Constantinople, and cannily took on unemployed mosaicists from the eastern capital for his own building projects, not least the extension and decoration of Sta Prassede. But Paschal

10. Torrance, "Ministry of Women: An Argument."

was in a difficult position. The Papacy had only recently come under the protection of the Franks, after a long (though often nominal) attachment to the Emperor in Constantinople (all papal documents continued to be dated by the regnal year of the eastern Emperor until 800). A Pope in what was already an awkward period of transition, Paschal was persuaded to anoint, as joint emperor, Louis's son Lothair, then his preferred successor—thereby, perhaps unwittingly, embroiling the Papacy in the dynastic confusion which was to result in the break-up of the Carolingian Empire.

There can be little doubt, moreover, that Paschal, was *persona non grata* at Constaninople—the Emperor Leo IV (775–80) was a convinced iconoclast and Paschal had refused to recognize his new appointee as Patriarch in succession to the iconodule, Nicephorus. The Papacy, as Leo III had determined by his coronation of Charlemagne on Christmas Day 800, was now wedded to the Carolingian settlement. Whatever his personal views (and we cannot even guess what they might have been), Paschal must have been aware of the prevailing Frankish attitude to the role of women in society and in the Church. Clovis's Salic Law (c. 511), which prevented female succession to land, titles, or fiefdoms, was alive and well in the empire of Louis the Pious. Theodulph of Orleans (789–818), in effect Charlemagne's imperial commissioner for ecclesiastical affairs, had only recently re-applied similar principles to the transmission of Church property. Theodulph was, at the same time, insistent that his priests should instill respect for church buildings—no use of the village church to store hay against the winter!—and in particular, that they should guard the sanctity of the *sacrarium* (the area around the altar). No woman was to enter it. There might be license for females, even female "monarchs," in the decadent east (where a woman had reigned from 797 to 802, and Charles's closest advisers had consequently deemed the throne of the Empire vacant), but things were different in Francia. This, in short, was not a context in which a Pope could have a bishop for his mother, and get away with it for very long. Torrance's nonchalant acceptance of Theodora as bishop ("but that does not seem to have been the case in this instance") owes a lot to a view of the eighth and ninth centuries—once deemed "The Dark Ages"—now long past. The era of armchair historians with sweeping generalizations and textbooks with bold arrows showing barbarian penetrations ended a while ago. As Chris Wickham puts it: "It is now possible to write a very different sort of early medieval history."[11] Text without context is no longer an option.

11. Wickham, *Inheritance of Rome*.

There is, it should be noticed, an added irony to this feminist enthusiasm for "Theodora Episcopa" which might easily go unremarked. Torrance, who seems to have given the mosaic (or a photograph of it) only a cursory glance, does not identify the three other women in the picture. They are (not surprisingly) the two joint patrons of the basilica (SS. Praxedis (Prassede) and Pudentia, her sister) and the Blessed Virgin. The original church on the site was built to house the tombs of those sister saints, whose father, the senator Pudens, was reputedly Peter's first convert in Rome. The site was one of the Roman tituli, or *ecclesie domesticae*. There, on the Esquiline Hill, the local church met and worshipped. From it the two sisters were taken by force and murdered for providing Christian burial for early martyrs, in defiance of Roman law. It seems that Paschal, in the course of an unprecedentedly lavish program of building works, gave Sta Prassede pride of place. He wanted to honor these Christian pioneers and be associated with them. In the chapel of S. Zeno, he portrayed his mother with her patrons. In the mosaics of the triumphal arch he himself is represented, bearing a model of the church. But pride of place, alongside the pillars of the Roman Church, Peter and Paul, is given to the sister martyrs, whom the Apostles are presenting to the risen Christ. They have, as the mosaic makes plain, a dignity far exceeding that of bishops or popes. The tragedy is that, in a vain search for a precedent for female ordination, people wanting to celebrate the heroic role of Christian women have instead created a fantasy—"Theodora the Bishop." And in doing so, they have turned their backs on the reality—the real women who gave their lives for Christ. Now, with the Holy Apostles, it is the martyred sisters and not "bishop" Theodora, the mosaics are telling us, who share Christ's triumph and his glory.

* * *

The story of Pope Joan—celebrated in a book[12] and television program by Peter Stanford ("As the furore over women in the catholic priesthood continues, and the Church, which once took her story as gospel, now tries to play down the rumours . . .")[13]—seems to have been too far-fetched even for Professor Torrance. The facts are far from simple, but they appear to be as follows.

12. Stanford, *She-Pope: Quest for Truth*.
13. Publisher's blurb for Stanford, *She-Pope: Quest for Truth*.

In 1265 a Dominican who had served as Papal chaplain under Clement IV produced what, in medieval terms, was a best-seller. In a single paragraph, Martin Polonus (he came from Troppau in Poland) gave the essentials of what was to become an enduring fable.

> After Leo, John, an Englishman born at Mainz, was Pope for two years, seven months and four days, and died in Rome, after which there was a vacancy in the papacy of one month. It is claimed that this John was a woman, who as a girl had been brought to Athens in the clothes of a man by a certain lover of hers. There she became proficient in a diversity of branches of knowledge until she had no equal; and afterwards in Rome, she taught the liberal arts and had great masters among her students and audience. In the city the opinion of her life and learning grew ever higher, and she was the unanimous choice for Pope. While Pope, however, she became pregnant by her companion. Through ignorance of the exact time when the birth was expected, she was delivered of a child while in procession from St. Peter's to the Lateran, in a narrow lane between the Colosseum and St. Clement's church. After her death, it is said that she was buried in that same place. The Lord Pope always turns aside from this street and it is believed by many that this is done because of abhorrence of the event. Nor is she placed on the list of the holy pontiffs, both because of her female sex and on account of the shamefulness of the event.[14]

Martin dates Pope Joanna between Leo IV and Benedict III, so around 855–57, but there is no general agreement. Jean de Mailly, another thirteenth century Dominican, dates her far later (1099–1016). Seven years is a long time successfully to pursue such a deception! Other authorities took up the tale and obviously enjoyed the retelling, among them Bartolomeo Platina, Prefect of the Vatican Library under Sixtus IV (1471–1484). The Bohemian reformer, Jan Hus, was only too pleased to revive the canard in his evidence before the Council of Constance (1414–15). (Needless to say, Hus was making a case, not for women Popes, but against the Papacy!) Rather confusingly, Hus called her Agnes. And it is as Agnes that she appears again in the travelogue of the Welshman, Adam of Usk, who wrote an account of Innocent VII's coronation in 1404. There was, he claims, a statue of her at the very point (probably on the Via San Giovanni in Laterano, near the church of San Clemente) where she was said to have given

---

14. Martin of Torppau, *Chronicum Pontificumet Imperatum*, cited in Norwich, *The Popes: A History*, 60.

birth. The most entertaining detail of the Joanna legend, however, is the *chaise percée*, a red porphyry seat which is said to have been used to ensure that subsequent Popes could not practice the same deception. According to Felix Haemerlein's *De Noblitatis et Rusticitata Dialogus* (c. 1490), before the election could be confirmed, a junior cleric was deputed to grasp the pontifical testicles through the hole in the chair.

Fascination with the tale seems to have increased throughout the fifteenth century and beyond.

> One enthusiastic writer, Mario Equicola of Alvito (near Caserta: d. 1525), even argued that Providence had used Joan's elevation to demonstrate the equality of women with men. Catholic criticism of the legend became increasingly vocal from the middle of the 16th cent., but it was a French Protestant, David Blondel (1590–1655), who effectively demolished it in treatises published at Amsterdam in 1647 and 1657.[15]

Needless to say, despite the refutation, it was taken up with alacrity by the *philosophes* of the Enlightenment, with whom any stick with which to beat the Catholic Church was welcome, and truth was seldom allowed to spoil a good story. In the eighteenth century, *Pope Joan* even became a popular card game. But the truth—if contemporary evidence is taken into account—leaves one in little doubt that the legend owes more to monkish prurience than to actual fact. Like the evidence already cited in the case of the lady Theodora, this dates from the period of antagonism between Rome and Constantinople in the aftermath of the iconoclast controversy and the establishment of the Western Empire. Photius, who was Patriarch of Constantinople from 858 to 865, would have been, according to Martin Polonus, Joan's exact contemporary, and therefore in routine correspondence with her. Photius, it need hardly be said, was no lover of the pretensions of Rome. He nevertheless casually refers to "Leo and Benedict, *successively* great priests of the Roman Church": no space there for a female interloper. More conclusive still is a letter from Leo IX (1049–54) to Patriarch Michael Cerularius.

> God forbid that we wish to believe what public opinion does not hesitate to claim has occurred in the Church of Constantinople: namely that in promoting eunuchs indiscriminately against the First Law of the Council of Nicaea, it once raised a woman on to the seat of its pontiff. We regard this crime as so abominable and

15. Kelly, *Oxford Dictionary of Popes*, 329.

horrible that although outrage and disgust and brotherly goodwill do not allow us to believe it, nevertheless, reflecting upon your carelessness towards the judgement of Holy Law, we consider that it could have occurred, since even now you indifferently and repeatedly promote eunuchs and those who are weak in some part of their body not only to clerical office, but also to the position of pontiff.[16]

Clearly neither Leo nor Michael Cerularius had heard of Pope Joan, or the correspondence would no doubt have taken an altogether more interesting turn!

The legend of Pope Joan, you might say, is hardly worth the ink I have expended upon it. But it is nevertheless a case in point. Of course every age delights in tales of intrigue and deception; and tour guides in every generation fabricate improbable explanations of untoward things or events to titillate their audience and eke out an otherwise threadbare narrative. Peter Stanford's television program, I suppose, was merely an intellectually pretentious sequel to the 1972 film starring Liv Ulman, Trevor Howard, and Olivia de Havilland. But why, even if it were true, should anyone suppose the imposture of a Dark Age transvestite to be an argument for the ordination of women? It is a question to be asked. And the answer is surely that there is a total and embarrassing absence of anything more convincing.

* * *

The three examples that make up the bulk of this chapter have a good deal in common. In the first place they all derive from an uncritical reading of Joan Morris's seminal book. Morris, it is apparent, was no scholar; but she had an eye for what was catching. In 1970 there was a revisionist wind already blowing. It was clear by the 1980s that almost any practice or opinion could be attributed to the Church of the first few centuries with virtual impunity. A one-man crusade by the American scholar James Boswell[17] attempted to do for homosexualism what was already well advanced for feminism.

> Through analysis of a multitude of induction ceremonies, contractual forms, covenants, oaths, blessings, arrangements for the disposition of property and other types of publicly testified and legally-morally binding unions, Boswell shows that Christendom

16. Cited in Norwich, *The Popes: A History*, 66.

17. Boswell, *Christianity, Social Tolerance*; Boswell, *Marriage of Likeness*.

has had a major homosexual past which weighty authorities during the last few 100 years have chosen to suppress or ignore.[18]

All that was required to gain for them an unwonted degree of credibility was to locate those attitudes and practices in far-flung places, at distant times, and among fringe communities.

The second thing the examples have in common is television. With rare exceptions it is bad history that makes good television. Televisual presentation of complex issues is necessarily sketchy and partisan. There is seldom more than an hour (with intermissions) to examine evidence and make a case. The audience, moreover, is seldom in a position to evaluate the reliability of the authorities whose opinions are canvassed. This makes television the ideal medium for presenting a revisionist view. It is usually portrayed as what "they" (the establishment experts) have been hiding from "us" (the duped majority). This fits well with the "hermeneutic of suspicion," which has long been part of the feminist armory. It is, of course, impossible to say how far programs like *The Hidden Tradition* and Peter Stanford's *She-Pope* may have influenced public opinion about women's ordination. The success of such programs depends on their ability to reinforce generally held attitudes, rather than to alter them. But they will certainly have given to doubtful evidence a spurious credibility. That, after all, was the aim.

The growth of literature claiming a variety of women ministers throughout the Mediterranean and from the earliest times has increased exponentially since Joan Morris. Several generations of undergraduates have now been taught that women deacons and presbyters were commonplace in the Pauline churches and throughout the region. Books making such claims are numerous enough to constitute a distinct genre, related to and in many ways dependent on other books about priestesses in the ancient world,[19] or about what is usually called "the goddess" or the "divine female."[20] Karen Torjesen[21] takes up and develops themes already rehearsed by Morris. *Women in the Early Church (Message of the Fathers of the Church)* by Elizabeth A. Clark (1992) is a useful collection of patristic citations intended to show a variety of attitudes to women in the church of the first five

---

18. Publisher's blurb for Boswell, *Christianity, Social Tolerance*; Boswell, *Marriage of Likeness*.

19. Of which the most accessible is probably Connelly, *Portrait of a Priestess*.

20. E.g., Harvey and Baring, *Divine Feminine*; Sjöö and Mor, *Great Cosmic Mother*; Gimbutas, *Language of the Goddess*.

21. Torjesen, *When Women Were Priests*.

centuries. Most of the works in the genre subscribe enthusiastically to the myth of the Fall into Patriarchy. They are confident that women's priestly ministry was eroded by misogyny or (more subtly) by the rise of asceticism (which these authors generally view with equivalent distaste). Gary Macy[22] has an altogether more sophisticated theory. He claims that "most scholars use a definition of ordination that would have been unknown in the middle ages." A change in the understanding of the meaning of "ordo" in the eleventh and twelfth centuries, he maintains, altered perceptions radically. The modern view that women were never ordained is "a premise based on false terms" (sic). A feature common to almost all these surveys (even that of Macy) is the blithe assumption that their findings are directly relevant to the contemporary situation.

Where epigraphical evidence is concerned, there is obviously a problem in determining to what group—"heretical" or "orthodox"—the women referred to belonged. Hard evidence, even for heretical groups, is sparse and doubtful. Kevin Madigan and Carolyn Osiek[23] have usefully compiled citations and translations of all the relevant texts—including inscriptions. There are maps showing the distribution of the evidence for both deacons and presbyters. The authors conclude:

> Most previous studies of female deacons have focused on the nature of their ordination and sacramental role, or lack thereof. We have given some consideration to this question, but we hope that by expanding the presentation of evidence, we can move beyond these juridical questions to a greater appreciation of these women for who they were and what they actually did. Certainly the evidence for women presbyters is far less, but it cannot be confined to fringe or "heretical" groups. The intriguing profile that emerges is the larger number of references in the West than in the East, in spite of the determined efforts of various councils to eliminate them.[24]

It is a triumph of optimism over data, as anyone who will take the trouble to read the book can ascertain. A significant amount of the evidence (as in their conclusion they tacitly admit) comes from the canons of those councils which sought to outlaw what was generally held, at the time, to be outrageous and unnatural. As the history of witch trials and anti-sorcery legislation in the early modern period is enough to demonstrate, it

22. Macy, *Hidden History of Women's Ordination.*

23. Madigan and Osiek, *Ordained Women in the Early Church.*

24. Ibid., 9.

is foolhardy indeed to conclude that because something was forbidden it must have been practiced.

What these attempts to demonstrate provenance for women's ordained ministry also have in common is the use of conspiracy theory. Wilpert, the "discoverer" of the Capella Graeca (or his water-colorist) was accused by Lavinia Byrne of deliberately seeking to conceal the sex of the figures he was painting—for no other reason than that he was a man. The inscription over the image of the Lady Theodora is said to have been defaced in a clumsy restoration (". . . but the 'a' on Theodora has been partly effaced by scratches across the glass tiles of the mosaic, leading to the disturbing conclusion that attempts were made to deface the feminine ending . . ."), so it must have been part of a deliberate attempt to eliminate her from history! The supposed failure to take seriously the "evidence" for Pope Joan is portrayed as part of a Vatican conspiracy (". . . the Church, which once took her story as gospel, now tries to play down the rumours . . .").

Though this assumption of conspiracy plays out well in the world of Dan Brown and *Holy Blood and Holy Grail*, it is by no means a modern phenomenon. Curiously, it was the Age of Reason that brought to birth the world's first rash of conspiracy theories. "Man is born free," wrote Rousseau, "and everywhere he is in chains." This sad decline from man's natural state of freedom and felicity demanded an explanation; and since the age-old wisdom of the Church ("for all have sinned and fall short of the glory of God" [Rom 3:23]) was no longer available, another explanation had to be found. *Some* men had sinned; and now, in an age of Enlightenment, they would *all* have their comeuppance. Marie Jean Antoine Nicolas de Caritat, Marquis de Condorcet, told his readers in his modestly titled *Sketch for an Historical Picture of the Progress of the Human Mind* (1794) that soon "the Great Religions of the Orient" (by which he meant most especially Christianity), which had for so long subjugated their adherents "in slavery without hope and perpetual infancy," would be shown up for the lies, tricks, and impostures that they were. Soon, "the sun will rise only upon a world of free men who will recognize no master other than their own reason, where tyrants and slaves, priests and their stupid or hypocritical instruments, will exist only in history or in the theatre." Diderot had put the matter rather more succinctly; but the sentiments were the same: all the ills of humankind were to be attributed to a conspiracy of priests and kings. They had contrived to keep the majority in ignorance and slavery for their own material advantage. (Condorcet's *Sketch*, alas, was never finished. In the very year that it was begun the forces of Enlightenment did for him what the universal conspiracy of priests and monarchs had failed to do. He died in prison on March 27, 1794, where paradoxically he had been incarcerated for his opposition to the regicide.)

If a worldwide conspiracy of the few against the many was the Enlightenment solution to the problem of mankind's descent from felicity, the opponents of the Enlightenment were not slow to repay the compliment. The precipitous fall of the *ancien régime*, and its apparent irreversibility, was for them an event so monstrous that it also required a dramatic explanation. In default of a serious analysis of ideas and events, conspiracy theories proliferated: freemasons, Illuminati, even (rather counter-intuitively) Jesuits.[25] *Someone*—some malevolent grouping—must have been responsible! It is not difficult to trace the lineal descent of fantasies about the assassination of John F. Kennedy, the death of Diana, Princess of Wales, and ultimately (and trivially) *The Da Vinci Code*. With the followers of Marx and Engels, conspiracy theory morphed into class warfare. And from there it was a short step to scapegoating an entire sex. It was easy to blame all mankind's ills on Patriarchy, especially since there had never existed an alternative social system for comparison.

There is something heroic about the feminist endeavor to put all the blame on men. But the same does not apply to the examples we have been looking at. There, something rather less dashing is going on. When the only evidence for a theory is the hermeneutic of suspicion generated by it, the sleight-of-hand comes very close to dishonesty. What impresses more than the dishonesty, however, is the triviality. Suppose for a moment (what is very far from probable) that the fresco in the Catacomb of Priscilla depicts a gathering of concelebrating women priests of the early second century. Suppose that documents were to emerge showing that Theodora was Bishop of Ostia (as Pope Joan's son was later rumored to be). And suppose that correspondence were to be uncovered in the archives of the Ecumenical Patriarchate showing that the Patriarch Photius was privy to Joan's secret and had no problem with a woman on the throne of St. Peter. What would all that mean; what would it amount to? Not, I think, very much.

The cornice of the nave, choir, and transepts of Siena Cathedral is decorated with the carved heads of Popes. There are one hundred and seventy of them. They begin with St. Peter at the center of the apse and continue clockwise until they reach Lucius III who died in 1185. Until about 1600

25. See Zamoyski, *Phantom Terror: Threat of Revolution*.

(when Clement VIII had her removed) there, sure enough, was *Johannes VIII, Foemina de Anglia*—the fabled Pope Joan ("an English woman"): one out of a hundred and seventy, and she a transvestite! The papal heads of Siena are a visual reminder of all those innumerable lists in cathedral chanceries across Europe, recording for posterity the episcopal succession upon which the authority and authenticity of the see depended (and therefore, of course, the sacraments celebrated within it). Not a woman among them! It is the same with early Christian art, in the catacombs and elsewhere. A catalogue of the most frequently recurring images from the Roman catacombs—Daniel in the lions' den, the Good Shepherd, Jonah, Lazarus, the sacrifice of Isaac—does not include women (even the Mother of God). If Patriarchy is indeed a crime, there is evidence enough to convict.

* * *

Christian feminists have long struggled with the intractable androcentricity of the Bible. Techniques have been developed to deal with it, not least in the work of Elizabeth Schüssler Fiorenza and Phyllis Trible. Trible sought to deal, not merely with the virtual invisibility of women in the scriptures, but with passages where women are thought to have been slandered or traduced. Writing with reference to Trible's work, Nicola Slee comments:

> I believe that it is possible for feminists to reclaim much of the biblical material in ways that enable us to celebrate and affirm and make sense of our own experience, without for a moment supposing that the biblical writers themselves (or even Jesus himself) would have intended the material to be understood in this way.[26]

Daphne Hampson perceptively responds:

> The efforts of Christian feminists to enable the scriptures to be accessible have been ingenious. Yet they never quite succeed. The central issue as to whether feminist insights can ever be squared with the biblical literature is for the most part dodged . . . One has the impression that women have taken a prior decision to be Christian, and, given that they are Christian, they do the best that can be done with the text . . . If one is actually talking about feminism, the equality of women and men, is Christianity ever going to be able to deliver the goods? For all the chipping away here, the re-reading there, the underlying problem remains. Christianity is

26. Letter to Daphne Hampson, cited in Hampson, *Theology and Feminism*, 105.

a historical religion which must needs have deep roots in a patriarchal past.[27]

Hampson's point is as relevant to the broader sweep of Christian history
and to the character of paleo-Christian iconography as it is to the study of
the scriptures. Quite simply: why clutch at straws? If the Judeo-Christian
scriptures are irredeemably patriarchalist, why privilege them? Why not
treat them like any other set of ancient texts? If the history of the earliest
Christians is one which, for all intents and purposes, excludes women and
renders them invisible, why give it status and authority? The most powerful argument advanced by the Catholic Church against women priests and
bishops is the argument from tradition: the past (scriptural precept and
Christian practice aggregated) does not permit the contemporary church
to arrogate to itself the authority for such a change. "Declaramus Eccle-
siam facultatem nullatenus habere ordinationem sacerdotalem mulieribus
conferendi" [We declare that the Church has no authority whatsoever to
confer priestly ordination on women].[28] That is because, for the Catholic Church, tradition is in every sense normative and definitive. Why, for
feminists (if the ethical imperative is to undo past wrongs) is the reverse
not the case? Why are they not obliged, by the same unvarying witness and
tradition, to abandon the attempt and (because it necessarily follows) the
religion? Nothing can possibly be gained by ineffectual tinkering with the
past and by the fabrication of evidence which, even if true, would be inconsequential. There can be no stronger argument for change, surely, than that
the past is intolerable.

27. Hampson, *Theology and Feminism*, 107.

28. John Paul II, "Ordinatio Sacerdotalis," apostolic letter, May 22, 1994.

7: Conclusions

*I have heard many arguments in favour of women's ordination,
but not yet a good one.*

—MONSIGNOR GRAHAM LEONARD

I t is clear that many, perhaps most, of the claims about the Christian past
routinely made by supporters of women's ordination are hopelessly opti-
mistic, if not downright fraudulent. There is no evidence that Jesus deviated
in any significant way from the mores of his contemporaries in his attitude
to women. Certainly he entertained no program for gender equality. The
Apostle Paul was no social revolutionary, in this or in anything else. His
priorities were preaching the gospel to the limits of the known world (to
hasten the coming of the Lord), and conforming his new Christian communities (in preparation for that event) to the teachings of Jesus as he, Paul,
had received them. Gender equality played no part in those teachings. Mary
Magdalen was not the first to see the risen Lord, and was not commissioned
by him to proclaim the resurrection. When the time came to make up the
number of the Twelve (men chosen to symbolize the twelve Patriarchs of
the Old Israel in the constitution of the New) she was not even considered.
Only a loose and variable usage of the term "apostle" (never impinging on
the unique status of "the twelve") has allowed her to be so-called. The Junias
mentioned in passing in the final paragraph of the Letter to the Romans
was not, with any degree of certainty, either a woman or an "apostle." The
evidence for women ministers of any kind among orthodox Christians in
the first two centuries is sparse and doubtful. The frescoes in the Catacomb
of Priscilla do not represent either a concelebration by women priests or
by Priscilla and Aquila together. The mother of Pope Pascal I was not a

bishop. "Pope Joan" was a prurient monkish fabrication, later adapted for use by Protestant propagandists. It seems that Graham Leonard's dictum ("I have heard many arguments in favour of women's ordination, but not yet a good one") holds true. So, if these are not they, what *are* the arguments for the ordination of women to the priesthood and the episcopate, and why have a majority in the Church of England (and elsewhere) found them convincing? In his opening contribution to the debate in the General Synod of the Church of England in November 1992 (described in *The Times* as a "disappointingly lacklustre speech"), Bishop Michael Adie came up with an ingenious formula. Women's ordination he claimed is "a reasoned development, consonant with Scripture, required by tradition."[1] It is a statement which rewards careful unpacking, for much is included or implied.

The basic structure of the formula—reason, scripture, tradition—is, of course, derived from what is usually referred to as "Hooker's three-legged stool." The idea has had a remarkable currency in recent debate about the nature of Anglicanism. What makes Anglicanism unique? An earlier generation of Anglicans replied, "Nothing at all. We are a 'bridge church' with a vocation to draw all churches together. We hold nothing that is distinct and uniquely Anglican; our beliefs and practices are simply those that are common to the church universal." More recently the answer has gone something like this: "Anglicans do not ascribe an absolute authority to Scripture. At the same time, Anglicanism rejects the absolute claims of an infallible papacy. Anglicanism is distinct in its reliance on the 'Three-Legged Stool' of Scripture, Reason, and Tradition." Attributed to the sixteenth century divine, Richard Hooker, the "Three-Legged Stool" has become the essential feature of a distinct "Anglican Ethos." Its popularity appears to lie in the manner in which it functions to exclude any form of religious absolutism. Neither the Bible, nor the authority of the Church, nor the reasoning intellect can claim the last word; but together they offer a balanced way to discern the will of God. The notion, moreover, has proved flexible and adaptable. Recently, and tellingly, "reason" has been replaced in some accounts by "contemporary experience"; and "tradition," as we will see in Adie's case, has been used very loosely indeed. But the basic idea remains: the three legs necessarily carry equal weight, or the stool would topple over. In the popular imagination it has become as substantial a piece of Tudor furniture as the Great Bed of Ware; but the truth is that Hooker himself never used the image. The

---

1. General Synod, *Ordination of Women: Synod Debate*, 9.

passage in the "Laws of Ecclesiastical Polity" from which the notion seems to derive reads thus:

> . . . what scripture doth plainly deliver, to that the first place of credit and obedience is due; the next whereunto is whatsoever any man can necessarily conclude by force of reason; after these the voice of the Church succeedeth. That which the Church by her ecclesiastical authority shall probably think and define to be true and good, must in congruity of reason overrule all other inferior judgements whatsoever.[2]

If the image of a stool suggests a balance of three equal components, for Hooker these three do not have equal standing. To Scripture, "first place both of credit and obedience is due," after which reason and ecclesiastical authority follow in an ordered sequence. Notice that for Hooker reason is not mere surmise, probability, or commonly agreed opinion. "Force of reason" requires logical necessity. He is wholly in agreement, it seems, with Article VI of the thirty-nine:

> Holy Scripture containeth all things necessary to salvation: so that *whatsoever is not read therein, nor may be proved thereby,* is not to be required of any man, that it should be believed as an article of the Faith, or be thought requisite or necessary to salvation.[3]

Of the sufficiency of scripture, Hooker himself writes:

> This we believe, this we hold, this the Prophets and Evangelists have declared, this the Apostles have delivered, this Martyrs have sealed with their blood, and confessed in the midst of torments, to this we cleave as to the anchor of our souls, against this though an Angel from heaven should preach unto us, we would not believe.[4]

Ecclesiastical authority, moreover, (the magisterium of the Church, as Catholics might style it) trumps the opinions of both an individual and a minority—"other inferior judgements whatsoever." They must be subordinate to it. There is something playful—satirical almost—in the way Adie adopts Hooker's idea simply in order to subvert it. We are dealing here with a mere rhetorical flourish, albeit delivered with a certain panache. It is intended to give a beguiling sixteenth-century patina to a confection of distinctly twentieth century novelties.

2. Hooker, *Laws of Ecclesiastical Polity,* vol. 2, book 5, sec. VII.2, p. 31.

3. *The Articles of Religion,* appended to *The Book of Common Prayer, 1571.*

4. Hooker, *Laws of Ecclesiastical Polity,* vol. 2, book 5, sec. VII.2, p. 30.

* * *

Nothing illustrates more clearly the distance between Adie and Hooker than the slippery phrase "consonant with scripture." In the course of the 1992 debate, Alec Graham, then Chairman of the Church of England Doctrine Commission, commented:

> He stated, if I heard him aright, that Scripture is inconclusive on the matter of the ordination of women. Surely Scripture never addresses that question? As far as I recollect, that precise question is never addressed. Then he claimed that the ordination of women to the priesthood is consonant with Scripture. We all know that to be a matter of opinion. There is argument enough about that, as we all know.[5]

Graham had, of course, "heard aright." The fact that scripture does not address the question raises problems of its own. If the ordination of women is (as the House of Bishops of the Church of England asserted) "intimately related" to the "centre of the faith"; and if, because Orders are instrumental in the administration of the sacraments, they are in that sense "requisite or necessary to salvation," then a *sola scriptura* approach, such as that of Hooker and Article VI, could never settle the matter. The ordination of women might remain a *theologoumenon*; but it could never become an established practice.

It is a useful exercise to consider the available alternatives to Adie's Hooker-esque formula. They are three—though one can see why he was unlikely to consider any of them very attractive in the circumstances.

He might have maintained that women's ordination was a "second order" issue, one like, for example, the celibacy of the clergy. He could have claimed that it was well within the competence of a particular local church. Conventions about orders, he might have claimed, may vary from place to place and from time to time without affecting in any way the common deposit of faith. Of course, to have done so would have involved contradicting the recent claims of the House of Bishops, which might be thought to carry some weight. But far more seriously, it would have been seen as belittling the significance of the proposed change. It would have looked as though he were ignoring the emotional intensity and righteous indignation which had fuelled the campaign. In short, it would have let the side down.

---

5. General Synod, *Ordination of Women: Synod Debate*, 40.

And—a secondary consideration, but politically significant—it would have been wholly unacceptable to the opponents.

He could, on the other hand, have said that women's ordination was fundamentally consistent with the core doctrines of the faith and necessary so that it could be preached with coherence and integrity in the modern world. He might have claimed it as a development less like clerical celibacy and more like the promulgation of the Marian dogmas in the Roman Church. The problems with such an approach, however, are two-fold. The first problem springs from the long history of antipathy to women's ordination. The Marian dogmas, whatever Anglicans might think of them, had long been widely held by many of the faithful. Their promulgation was the conclusion of a process of reception. Not so with women's ordination. If, by the feminists' own account, women priests were ubiquitous in the early church, but had effectively been eliminated by the third or fourth centuries, then we have a clear example of a development which had *not* been "received." The second problem arises from the genius of Anglicanism itself. There is a problem in seeking to impose dogma of any kind on Anglicans. Language about the Church of England being a "bridge church," a "broad church," even an "inclusive church," makes requiring belief in anything beyond the deposit already received a very doubtful proceeding.

A third possibility was that Adie might have cast aside concern for scripture and tradition altogether and simply claimed that women's ordination was a matter of basic justice. Such an ethical *a priori* position would treat women's ordination as essentially the same as other consequences of a belief in the absolute equality of the human species—like universal suffrage. The innovation would then stand in need of no precedent. Indeed, to seek to defend it from scripture and tradition would be an absurdity: what is self-evidently the case cannot be supposed to be subject to the arbitration of ancient literature and the conduct of ages long past.

Many advocates of the ordination of women would, in the event, probably have preferred Adie to have adopted such an approach. But with at least one house of the General Synod balanced on a knife-edge, and opposition in the Church at large running at around 30 percent, it was clearly not a viable political option. To alienate possible marginal support would have been to court near certain defeat. There were, moreover serious ecumenical disadvantages. An ethical *a priori* position would have subjected to moral opprobrium the majority of living Christians and all dead ones.

Small wonder, then, when the alternatives were so fraught with difficulty that the bishop placed his faith in an ingenious re-engineering of Hooker's mythical stool, and in a dilution of Hooker's insistence on the plain meaning of scripture to almost homeopathic proportions.

* * *

"Consonant with scripture." In order to supply the scriptural deficit pointed out by Alec Graham, Michael Adie enlisted a particular exegesis of Genesis 1:26–27 and a particular theory of the *imago dei:*

> The profound truth of the Bible with regard to men and women is that both men and women are made in the image of God. That is the fundamental truth of Genesis, picked up by Jesus (according to the gospels) and alluded to by St. Paul in his letter to the Galatians: man and woman are complementary to one another, equal but distinct partners, and together they make up humanity fit for friendship with God. That fundamental scriptural truth remains whichever way our vote goes today. If woman has been regarded or treated as subservient to man, that is because of our human failure, that twisting of God's purpose which we call the Fall. St. Paul may well be unclear on the place of women in the Church but that is because he is wrestling with making sense of our failure to grasp the divine truth of man and woman together being in the image of God. The Scriptures are inconclusive on the question of the ordination of women; they are firm and conclusive on man and woman together being in the image of God.[6]

This creative use of texts deserves comment. Three texts in the Hebrew bible refer to the image of God:

> **Gen 1:26–27**: And God said: Let us make mankind in our image/*b'tsalmeinu*, as our likeness/*kid'muteinu*. And they will have dominion over [the animals] . . . And God created humankind in His image/*b'tsalmo*, in God's image/*tselem* he created him, male and female he created them. And God blessed them and God said to them: Be fruitful and multiply, and fill the land and occupy it, and have dominion over the sea's fish and the skies' bird and every animal crawling over the land.

---

6. General Synod, *Ordination of Women: Synod Debate*, 9–10.

Gen 5:1–3: This is the book of Adam's generations: On the day God created Mankind, in God's likeness/*d'mut* he created him; male and female he created them, and he blessed them, and called their name Adam in the day of their being created. And Adam lived a hundred and thirty years and bore in his likeness/*bid'muto* like his image/*k'tsalmo* and called his name Seth.

Gen 9:6: One who spills the blood of man, through/by man, his blood will be spilled, for in God's image/*tselem* he made man.

The last uses the notion to sanction capital punishment. The other two are susceptible to various interpretations. Jesus himself, it should be noted (Matt 19:4; Mark 10:6) (*pace* Adie) does not use the Genesis texts to demonstrate the *equality* of women and men, but rather to *forbid divorce*. There is, moreover, no reference at all to the *imago dei* in the letter to the Galatians, where, according to Adie, Paul was "wrestling with making sense of our failure to grasp the divine truth of man and woman together being in the image of God"—though one can see, considering the importance of Galatians 3:28 as a slogan in the campaign, why he might have wished it to be otherwise.

An interesting characteristic of these texts is the variable use of the term *adam (man)*. It is sometimes deployed as a collective noun (here rendered "mankind") and sometimes as a personal name. So "Adam" generates "Seth"—no mention, notice, of the female offspring who must logically have existed. In the line of transmission, the female, it appears, was largely irrelevant.[7] For modern exegetes, this poses something of a problem; but there was no apparent problem for the early redactors of the texts in question. They wholeheartedly embraced the principle (anathema to modern feminists) that the male includes the female. The New Testament writers took up that same principle and developed it. The *imago* in the New Testament is generally applied to Jesus, the second Adam:

> **Heb 1:3** — God, having in the past spoken to the fathers through the prophets at many times and in various ways, has at the end of these days spoken to us by his Son, whom he appointed heir of all things, through whom also he made the worlds. His Son is the radiance of his glory, the very image of his substance.

7. Cf. the genealogies in Matthew and Luke, where the names of the foremothers are conspicuous by their (virtual) absence; a fact which is the more remarkable since Luke is obliged to point out that Jesus is not, as a matter of fact, the son of Joseph, the son of Hopi!

Col 1:13–15 — and translated us into the Kingdom of the Son of his love; in whom we have our redemption, the forgiveness of our sins; who is the image of the invisible God, the firstborn of all creation.

1 Cor 11:7 — For a man ought not to have his head covered, since he is God's image and glory; but the woman is the glory of the man.

Rom 8:29 — Because those whom he foreknew, he also predestined to be conformed to the image of His Son, that he might be the Firstborn among many brothers.

2 Cor 3:18 — But we all with unveiled face, beholding and reflecting like a mirror the glory of the Lord, are being transformed into the same image from glory to glory, even as from the Lord Spirit.

2 Cor 4:4–7 — that the light of the Gospel of the glory of Christ, who is the image of God, should not dawn on them. For we don't preach ourselves, but Christ Jesus as Lord, and ourselves as your servants for Jesus' sake; seeing it is God who said, "Light will shine out of darkness," who has shone in our hearts, to give the light of the knowledge of the glory of God in the face of Jesus Christ.

The *imago dei* has been variously understood throughout Christian history. There are three distinct modes: the substantive, the relational, and the functional. Some suppose that the image is a resemblance—spiritual rather than physical—which can be marred or lost. The medieval theologians, for the most part, thought that the image was impaired by the Fall. The Reformers generally agreed. Luther, in Article 114 of the Large Catechism, states that "Man lost the image of God when he fell into sin." Others suppose that the image subsists in the human capacity to make relationships, with God and with each other. Karl Barth and Emil Brunner, for example, argue that it is our ability to establish and maintain complex and intricate relationships that make us like God. In human beings the created order of male and female is intended to culminate in spiritual as well as physical union, reflecting God's nature and image. Since other creatures do not form such explicitly referential spiritual relationships, they see this ability as uniquely representing the *imago dei* in humans. A third group thinks that the image resides in the shared sovereignty with God which mankind exercises over creation (Gen 1:26).

It was with the Enlightenment, and in particular in the work of John Locke, that the *imago* came, for the first time, to be associated with human equality, and in particular with the equality of the sexes. Locke is famously inconsistent on the matter ("I conclude, therefore, that Locke's theory does display unequivocally sexist assumptions," says the feminist writer Lorenne Clark[8]), but the text of the First Treatise of Government does seem to argue sexual equality based on a functional view of the *imago*.

> God in this Donation, gave the World to Mankind in common, and not to Adam in particular. The word Them in the Text must include the Species of Man, for 'tis certain Them can by no means signifie Adam alone . . . They then were to have Dominion. Who? even those who were to have the Image of God, the Individuals of that Species of Man that he was going to make, for that Them should signifie Adam singly, exclusive of the rest, that should be in the World with him, is against both Scripture and all Reason: And it cannot possibly be made Sense, Man in the former part of the Verse do not signifie the same with Them in the latter, only Man there, as is usual, is taken for the Species, and them the individuals of that Species . . . God makes him in his own Image after his own Likeness, makes him in intellectual Creature, and so capable of Dominion. For whereinsoever else the Image of God consisted, the intellectual Nature was certainly a part of it, and belong'd to the whole Species.[9]

This diligent pursuit of pronouns leads Locke to conclude that Sir Robert Filmer (against whom he was writing) had got it wrong, and that the Genesis account of the prior creation of Adam did not give the male precedence or authority, as Filmer supposed. Locke even points out that if mere priority of creation established dominance and authority, then the animals must have the upper hand! What Locke's thesis does not rule out, however, is a diversity of roles and functions among human beings themselves. Men and women are equal in their proprietorial relationship to the rest of creation; but room is left for difference of status and function between them. Locke was, notoriously, an upholder of the sovereignty of the husband in marriage.[10] He has been criticized by feminist writers for failing to follow through the logic of his position; but not so. His argument is carefully constructed to leave open the possibility of male dominance. "Anyone who

8. Clark, L., "Women and Locke," 35.

9. Locke, *First Treatise on Government*, para. 30.

10. Locke, interestingly cites 1 Cor 11:7 as evidence.

reads the *Two Treatises on Government*," writes Jeremy Waldron, "alert to their religious and theological character, will find it striking how much is made of the Old Testament sources, and how little of any teaching or doctrine from the Christian Gospels or Epistles."[11] The good reason for that, as we have seen, is that there are no New Testament references to the equality of women and men. Indeed the consistent reference of the *imago dei* to the *imago Christi* in the Pauline letters must have been awkward for Locke. It is a good deal more embarrassing for modern Christian feminists.

Locke, of course, stands at the very end of a long tradition, beginning with Irenaeus of Lyons, which seeks to derive contemporary social practice from ancient biblical texts. But the attempt to base political theory on a strictly Biblical anthropology would soon come to seem old hat. Even in Locke's day, modern experimental science was driving it to the margins, where it remains. Man was coming to be seen as a self-constituting autonomous subject, apart from any relationship with God. From then on it was but a short step to the world of Feuerbach, Marx, and Freud, where it is not man who is made in the image of God, but God who is nothing else than an image projected by man. There is something endearingly quaint about Adie's belated attempt to ground in texts of scripture a doctrine of equality which they do not support and which is in fact alien to them.

"Consonant with scripture"? It is of course true that nowhere in scripture is the language of those three enigmatic references in Genesis in any way contradicted. But it is also true that nowhere in scripture does the interpretation placed upon them by Locke and Adie gain any explicit support. Nor do the Fathers support it. In recent Catholic theology, moreover, other themes have come to the fore. The Constitution on the Church in the Modern World (*Gaudium et Spes*) of the Second Vatican Council, and Saint John Paul II in the Apostolic Exhortation *Familiaris Consortio*, emphasise respectively the Christological and nuptial dimensions of the *imago*. Neither of these, of course, is particularly congenial to sexual egalitarians.

> In reality it is only in the mystery of the Word made flesh that the mystery of man truly becomes clear . . . Christ fully reveals man to himself and brings to light his most high calling.[12]

> Created in the image of God, human beings are called to love and communion. Because this vocation is realized in a distinctive way

11. Waldron, *God, Locke and Equality*, 188.

12. Paul II, *Gaudium et Spes*, 22.

in the procreative union of husband and wife, the difference between man and woman is an essential element in the constitution
of human beings made in the image of God.[13]

* * *

"Required by tradition." That was an astounding claim. How could a development which had played no part in the tradition (or rather, as feminists assert, was self-consciously rejected by it) be said now to be required?
Bishop Alec Graham responded at some length:

> Then he claimed that it was required by tradition. That really is
> quite a claim. He conceded that ordination of women to the priest-
> hood is not required by tradition in the sense that it has never
> happened before, but tradition is not just doing what has always
> been done before—an ever heavier load of practices and prohi-
> bitions. The Bishop maintained that ordination of women to the
> priesthood is demanded by the truth, required by the truth, as it
> has been handed down to us. If he had said it was demanded by
> the contemporary world, that is certainly often maintained and,
> we should all agree, is arguable. But surely it is not correct to say
> that tradition requires this development, for in this context tra-
> dition is the expression of the mind of the Church as set down
> in Scripture, interpreting, moulding, shaping the understanding
> of Scripture and of the mind of God revealed there, influenced
> by the contemporary world, tested by mind and conscience and
> tested against the original deposit. Tradition is set forward by the
> interplay between Scripture, the received mind of the Church, to-
> day's world and today's church members. That I understand to be
> the nature of tradition in this context. Surely it is quite misleading
> to enlist tradition without qualification in favour of this legisla-
> tion, for it is at this very point that the arguments in favour of the
> legislation are at their weakest. I hope that the Synod will not be
> beguiled by the Bishop of Guildford in this respect, for he begs the
> question whether this is a legitimate development of the tradition
> at this stage in our Church's life. The answer to that, I submit, is
> either "not proven" or a straight "no."[14]

13. John Paul II, *Familiaris Consortio*, 11.
14. General Synod, *Ordination of Women: Synod Debate*, 41.

Graham, of course, was merely restating Hooker's understanding of the role of tradition. In a short unscripted intervention in the debate, he was unable to address the important and specific claims being made about the implications of the doctrine of the Incarnation to which Adie was alluding.

Sometime in the late seventies of the last century a long-standing scholarly consensus began to be challenged. No one doubted that there had been women ministers among the Valentinians and other Gnostic groups; but it had been generally held that these were rejected by Catholics, who associated them with heretical beliefs and practices in other areas. Now there was a change of emphasis. This revisionist attempt did not seek to provide new and incontrovertible historical evidence, but rather to demonstrate that the anthropology and Christology of the Fathers was "inclusive" in a way which logically required the ordination of both women and men. A phrase of St. Gregory Nazianzen was adopted as a slogan: "Not taken; not healed." Jesus, it was claimed, could only save both men and women if the humanity assumed at the incarnation was inclusive of both. The aim was to wrong-foot opponents of women's ordination by showing that the proponents, not they, were the upholders of orthodoxy and tradition. It was a bold move, which rapidly gained support.

"If it is not inclusive humanity that is taken up into the Godhead then what implication does that have for the salvation of half the human race?" asked some of the bishops of the Church of England, in their second report on women's ordination (GS 829), for "what he did not assume he did not heal."[15] To say that only a male can represent Christ at the altar, Archbishop George Carey told the *Reader's Digest*, is "a most serious heresy," "devastating and destructive."[16] Tom Torrance went further: it was "sinning against the great soteriological principle of the Catholic and Apostolic Church."[17] This was theological over-kill, as opponents were not slow to point out; and it had obvious and serious ecumenical implications.[18] Three things need to be said in response:

The first is to point out that none of the Fathers to whom Professor Richard Norris refers (for it was his seminal article on which these claims were largely based) ever drew from this supposed anthropological and Christological consensus the conclusion which Norris himself draws.

15. GS 829, *Ordination of Women: Second Report*.

16. *Reader's Digest*, March 1991.

17. Letter in *The Sunday Times*, March 20, 1994.

18. See Catholic Church, *Catechism of the Catholic Church*, 1544–53, 1575.

Whatever their language might be thought to imply, the fact is that they did not ordain women (or ever advocate their ordination). They may have talked *something like* the talk; but they never walked the walk. That, of itself, should surely give pause for thought. It certainly does not encourage one to proclaim, as Michael Adie did on November 11, 1992, that "tradition" requires such an innovation.

The second is to point out that Norris's argument is one which purports to depend upon the Fathers; but to which the Fathers are largely irrelevant. It is entirely circular—and scarcely patrisitic at all. It depends not upon a patristic worldview, but upon the modern feminist axiom that for the male to include or represent the female is in some way offensive or inadmissible. The latter is mere assertion based on little more than sentiment, and needs to be challenged head-on. Is to say that "the maleness of the incarnation is not soteriologically significant" to say anything more than that "Jesus saves both women and men"? And if so, what?

The Fathers, of course, make nothing of the "maleness" of Jesus (as Norris puts it) for the simple reason that they had no problem with a male human being representing (or saving) a female. That was the inescapable assumption of their age. It was a view in which, as we have seen, scripture confirmed them. The only axiom which mattered to them was that Jesus Christ, the son of Mary, the Son of David, saves us all; a truth which they ever proclaimed. With Paul (Romans 8:22), they held that the whole of creation is redeemed in Christ. It never occurred to them that the "maleness" of Jesus might inhibit his saving power for all mankind, any more than that his "humanness" might prevent him from healing the whole natural world, animate and inanimate. Professor Norris, then, was asking the Nazianzen to address a problem which Gregory could scarcely have recognized as such. What fun to be a fly on the wall of eternity, overhearing the learned American professor repeatedly attempting to explain to the wily oriental ecclesiastic that his simple aphorism, "not taken; not healed," had implications to which he had been tragically blind, implications which damned as Christological heretics all Gregory's predecessors and contemporaries— and every Pope and Patriarch since!

Lastly, we need to read the recently coined slogan, not from a modern feminist perspective, but in its historical context. The second letter to Cledonius (from which the quotation comes) was written to a priest who had embraced the heresy of Apollinarius. Cledonius was maintaining that Christ did not possess a "rational mind." But, says Gregory later in the letter, "If Christ had not been endowed with a rational mind, how could he have been a man?" In order to save humans, says Gregory, Jesus had to be a man exactly as other men are. The Incarnation could not have been in any sense special, exceptional, or tailor-made. Had he shared Norris's view that Jesus's humanity in some sense "included" femaleness as well as maleness— in a way in which the humanity of other men (for example, male priests) does not—he would obviously have conceded the very point he was striving to defend. By citing Gregory out of context, Norris has conveniently misrepresented him.

Viewing all this dispassionately, the non-specialist observer might be confused. How, in any case, could a fourth century Byzantine be expected to share the presuppositions about sex and gender of a twentieth century East Coast American? The same observer would also probably raise an eyebrow at the thought that the humanity of Jesus, rather than his divinity, is the major problem for Christology in the twenty-first century. He might be moved to ask other questions as well. How widespread, in any case, are the largely Western presuppositions which undergird Norris's and Adie's assertions? Has the axiom that the male cannot represent the female really achieved universal acceptance in the modern world?

* * *

Bishop Michael Adie's strong suit was that a radical change had recently come about in the ambient culture.

> For centuries we have accepted men in the priesthood as the automatic consequence of God taking human nature, but then for centuries it was only men who enjoyed education, political leadership, the vote and so on, and these have only gradually, even grudgingly, become available to women. What God has made clear to us in our century is that women are not inferior to men, nor are they identical; men and women are complementary; together and equally they make up humanity. That simple but fundamental truth which God has shown to us in his world now resonates with a renewed understanding of the Scriptures.[19]

There is something naively self-congratulatory about this catalogue of improvements in education, political leadership, and the right to vote. What

19. General Synod, *Ordination of Women: Synod Debate*, 10.

precisely has God "made clear to us in our century" which was not clear to the church in the age of Catherine of Siena or of Teresa of Avila?

Here, one suspects, it is "the vote," that counts. The campaign for women's ordination in the Church of England had its roots in the suffragette movement. Its greatest synodical advocate, Christian Howard (who wrote three of the early papers on the subject—for the Church Assembly and later the General Synod), was the granddaughter of a leading suffragette. All the same, it is not immediately clear what is the supposed connection between universal suffrage and Christian ordination. Democracy and Christianity are not joined at the hip. Democracy has predominated in much of Europe and North America during rather less than a tenth of the lifespan of the church, and during most of that time suffrage was everywhere limited on grounds of social status, sex, or the ownership of property. The right to vote is only one (rather limited) expression of the belief in basic human equality. Equality itself is a rather slippery concept. How to define it and how to achieve it? Most discussion of the subject by philosophers and political theorists is big on the second question—on equality as an aim or matter of policy, on what contemporary political discourse rather loosely calls "fairness." But what sort of equality should we be striving to achieve (supposing that it is something to be aimed for at all)? Do we mean equality of wealth, equality of income, equality of opportunity, equality before the law? These distributive or policy questions raise others. Is "equality" merely emotive code language for something else, like the mitigation of poverty? And if it were definable and achievable, could it possibly remain stable?

Locke, who is remarkable among philosophers in tackling the subject of equality head-on (not "what to do?" but "what is it based on?") was a major influence, of course on the most famous statement of the principle:

> We hold these truths to be self-evident, that all men are created equal, that they are endowed by their Creator with certain unalienable Rights, that among these are Life, Liberty and the pursuit of Happiness . . .[20]

But the fact remains that very little work has been done on the nature of equality-in-itself. Strange, but true, that hardly any attention has been given to the problem of what, if anything, evokes it in the species it proposes to treat as equals. And what precisely would be involved in denying it. Perhaps in a world where human equality is taken as self-evident, it is simply bad

20. "American Declaration of Independence," in Krammnick, *Portable Enlightenment Reader*, 448–451.

form to question it. But what would have to be refuted in an argument against those who rejected it? And what, to put it another way, might be the criteria for deciding that one society is "more equal" than others?

Paradoxically, it seems that even in this secular age, the best answers to these difficult questions appear to be religious ones. In John Locke's view, the matter could easily be settled by reference to creation by God and to the God-given differentiation of species. Men are equal because equally created by God and equally answerable to him; the animals are not equal because subjected to man by God. So far so good, that is of course, if you are a Deist with an inclination to take Genesis more or less literally. But Locke lived a long time ago. Nowadays the majority of people are not so inclined. One wonders, for example, how many members of Parliament or Congress would feel obliged to decide public policy, on other matters (homosexuality for example), on the strength of an Old Testament text. We have entered an era in which, even for many Christians, the Bible has authority only when it can be made to seem in agreement with the ethical *a priori* assumptions of the contemporary world.

Bishop Adie, nevertheless, was confident that he could appeal to scripture to establish the equality of the sexes; that we would all know what equality was and what it required of us; and that we would conclude that office in the Church, like "political leadership," should therefore be open to all. None of this is as obvious or as straightforward as he tried to make it seem. The notion of equality, as we have seen, is a mine-field of provisos and qualifications; and the assumption that orders in the church can readily be equated with "political leadership" is unwarranted. It seems to be based on the rather crude notion that, as it is commonly put, "the priesthood represents God to the people and the people to God." But whilst the priesthood is certainly representative, as claimed, things are not quite so straightforward. The "representation" is not of a group (in the way in which Parliament "represents" the nation); it is direct and personal. The priest represents God and the people of God only because he represents Christ the Head and only mediator between God and men. This personal mode of representation (*in persona Christi capitis*[21]) poses once again the fundamental question: if a male priesthood cannot adequately or appropriately represent the whole people of God, how can Jesus? How does his humanity differ from theirs?

---

21. Catholic Church, *Catechism of the Catholic Church*, 1548.

* * *

Bishop Michael Adie's opening speech to the Synod may have been described as "lacklustre" by the correspondent of *The Times*, but it served a purpose. It was designed to make the innovation, which opponents had been characterizing as extreme and radical—"a new religion" in C. S. Lewis's memorable phrase—seem modest, reasonable, and above all Anglican. It needed to do so because the real arguments in favor, which emerged in two relatively short speeches later in the debate, were quite different.

The first speech came from the newly appointed Archbishop of Canterbury, George Carey. Eager no doubt to avoid the accusations leveled against his predecessor, of "nailing his colours to the fence,"[22] Carey was, in the words of *The Daily Telegraph*, "unexpectedly partisan." He was one of those who believed women's ordination to be merely a second order issue. He told Michael De-la-Noy as much in an interview in 1993:

> I don't think it will alter the Church of England fundamentally at all. I view the ordination of women as being an element of Church order rather than a fundamental shift in faith. I hear the phrase "a new orthodoxy" and I get impatient with that. There's no new orthodoxy about it. I've long been a student of ecclesiology and I'm sure that issues of ministerial order are secondary matters. They don't belong to the deposit of faith found in the creeds, so with the ordination of women there will be no constitutional alterations of the Church of England's faith.[23]

But that was not the theme of his speech in 1992. He spoke, instead, to the deep anxiety which had troubled the Anglican conscience throughout the second half of the twentieth century. In absolute (rather than percentage) terms, Church of England attendance figures peaked around the early sixties. From then on there was a precipitate decline, which has continued to the present day. It was a fact which, rather irritatingly to churchmen, featured in almost every news item about the church, in the press or on television. Their anxiety was about "relevance." The great "causes" in the second half of the twentieth century—Methodist reunion, liturgical revision, women's ordination—were always linked to these fears of precipitate decline and to the need to reverse it. Other churches, of course, have suffered a decline in numbers; but none is so affected by it as the Established

22. Attributed to Frank Field, MP.
23. De-la-Noy, *Church of England*, 303.

Church, which has to defend, in numerical terms, its privileged status and its bishops in the House of Lords. "Bums on pews" is how it is sometimes irreverently put. Carey saw the ordination of women primarily in that context.

> We must draw on all available talents if we are to be a credible church engaged in mission and ministry to an increasingly confused and lost world. We are in danger of not being heard if women are exercising leadership in every area of our society's life save the ordained priesthood.[24]

It would be difficult to overestimate the pressure on an established Church not to get out of step. In a more recent but not unrelated controversy, the Dean of York, the Very Reverend Vivienne Faull, spoke of the attitude of the House of Bishops of the Church of England to homosexual marriage. She said that increasing numbers of people—especially women—were recognizing the possibility of same-sex couples marrying. "That's a very significant change, and I am not sure that the House of Bishops has got that . . . it's very difficult for leaders of organisations to be right in touch with how quickly things are changing in the country."[25] It is clear from Dean Faull's comments that arguments like George Carey's for women's ordination will also be a deciding factor in forthcoming disputes. The scramble for relevance goes on.

The other speech was by Roy Williamson, at that time bishop of the radical diocese of Southwark. Far bolder than Michael Adie, he spoke of the issue in terms of basic justice: it was, for him an ethical *a priori* imperative which the danger of schism and of the possible alienation of fellow Christians did not outweigh.

> Of all the arguments opposing the ordination of women to the priesthood, and as one who was called to maintain the unity of the Church, I feel the weight of the sincerely held conviction of many that because of the threat to the unity of the Church the time may not yet be right; but as a seeker first of the Kingdom, I feel that if there is injustice to be removed the only time to do it is now. It is a risk I am prepared to take, casting myself on the mercy of God which, when you think of it, is something we all have to do at the end of the day and at the end of time.[26]

24. General Synod, *Ordination of Women: Synod Debate*, 23.

25. Quoted in *The Daily Telegraph*, April 29, 2014.

26. General Synod, *Ordination of Women: Synod Debate*, 63.

The religious affairs correspondents in the gallery where I was sitting were convinced he had nailed it: this was the moment, just into the afternoon of a long debate, which would seal the issue. The Revd. (now Monsignor) John Broadhurst, who spoke next, thought so too. "That last speech was a very powerful one, but I must say to the bishop that justice is only done if we give what God wants given, and that is the question we must grapple with and not our contemporary views of what may or may not be just."[27] They were words out of season: the majority could not—would not—hear them.

The impact of those two speeches, taken together, was what carried the day. And, in truth as it now seems, they expressed the emerging mind of the Church of England. Institutional neurosis and righteous indignation, taken together, are powerful emotions. Together, in this matter, they were conclusive. The rest, one is tempted to say, is mere persiflage. The attempt to find, in the dark recesses of the Book of Genesis, notions nowhere brought to light before the seventeenth century; the supposed special tenderness of Jesus toward women; the supposed internal struggle of Paul to express a radical vision realized only two millennia later; the supposed injustice done to the poor Magdalen, whose apostolic status a cabal of misogynists had conspired to suppress; the supposed distortion of the doctrine of the Incarnation by a church which should have been proclaiming it; the imagined ministry of the countless women allegedly air-brushed out of history: beside the claims of those two speeches—that action was needed in order to reverse decline, and must be taken because justice demanded it—all else was hardly significant.

A speech that passed almost unnoticed in the course of the debate was that of David Lunn, then Bishop of Sheffield.

> The supporters of the legislation are divided on this issue of revelation, perhaps more than they realise. Some (the majority, I suspect, though we have not heard much from them on this matter today) . . . do not believe that there is a revelation with a given, known, tangible, authoritative content: the Holy Spirit leads us without embarrassing encumbrance from the past. Others, while believing in the reality of God's revealed truth, have convinced themselves that the revelation is silent on this "indifferent" matter of ministry. Oh, my deaf friends, hear me. If this legislation is approved this afternoon the authority of Scripture in the decision-making processes of the Church of England will have been inexorably and fatally weakened. Let me speak particularly to the House of Bishops.

27. Ibid.

The bishops are appointed to be the guardians of that faith once delivered to us. To me it is both astonishing and distressing that the first fruits of the coming to prominence of so many Evangelicals among the bishops has been the steady carrying forward of this profoundly—at best—a-scriptural and very probably unscriptural legislation. All of you, laywomen, laymen, deacons, presbyters, bishops, who believe that there is a concrete reality in God's revelation of himself, and that this is guarded, lived and handed on in Scripture and in the life of the Church, must hesitate for a very long time indeed before you vote for this legislation which, however its supporters may decorate it with quotations from Scripture, has its roots in a very different system of belief.[28]

It was a speech that, in the eccentricity of its delivery, lost the impact it should have had. But it is packed with phrases prophetic of the future of the Church of England. "The Holy Spirit leads . . . without embarrassing encumbrance from the past." "The authority of scripture in the decision-making processes of the Church of England will have been inexorably weakened and fatally flawed." "This legislation, however its supporters may decorate it with quotations from scripture, has its roots in a very different system of belief."

Time has tested and proved the sagacity of those remarks. Though the Church of England continues, twenty years on, to celebrate the pain of those women who felt themselves denied their rights, the wisdom or otherwise of the innovation will be seen, not in its immediate fruits—the ministry of those women—but in the residual ability to deal with the social and ethical challenges which lie ahead. The immediate issue is that of homosexual marriage. No one in 1992, I suspect, envisaged a Conservative Party which would initiate changes in the understanding of marriage which would radically challenge the *ipsissima verba* of Jesus, the immemorial teaching of the Church, and the global cultural consensus of many millennia. But Vivienne Faull is right: "things are changing quickly in the country." And David Lunn was also right: the scriptural resources in the decision-making processes of the Church have been fatally weakened. (Michael Adie, you will recall, cited Jesus's own words about marriage, not to defend marital fidelity between a man and a woman—the burden of the texts—but to uphold a doctrine of sexual equality, which cannot be inferred from them.) It is not difficult to predict what the outcome will be. The real arguments in favor of women's ordination—anxiety about relevance and an un-nuanced attachment to

28. Ibid., 60–61.

justice and human rights—makes the embrace of same-sex marriage only a matter of time. The present Archbishop of Canterbury has said as much. The church will be seen as "increasingly irrelevant," Justin Welby told the General Synod, and as promoting attitudes "akin to racism."[29] On another (and, some had maintained, unrelated) topic he has nothing better to say than George Carey.[30]

David Lunn was also right about the origins of these ideas: "legislation which, however its supporters may decorate it with quotations from Scripture, has its roots in a very different system of belief." The language of inalienable and self-evident rights is very far from the unvarying vocabulary of the scriptures, which speak of divine will and gracious gift. It is the language of Jean-Jacques of Geneva, not of Jesus of Nazareth.

29. General Synod, "February [2014] Group of Sessions," 160.

30. In an interesting development in 2015, the image of Dr. Carey was removed from the windows of his old college (King's London) at the behest of homosexual activists on grounds of homophobia. Opposing recently introduced "equal marriage," Carey had opined: "It seems to me that so many of our current problems revolve around the all-too narrow attempt to make equality the controlling virtue. Acceptance of differences does not challenge equality. We are not the same."

Bibliography

"The American Declaration of Independence." In *The Portable Enlightenment Reader*, edited by Isaac Krammnick, 448–51. New York: Penguin, 1995.

Armstrong, Karen. *The End of Silence: Women and Priesthood*. London: Fourth Estate, 1993.

Astell, Mary. "Some Reflections on Marriage." In *The Portable Enlightenment Reader*, edited by Isaac Krammick, 484–531. New York: Penguin, 1995.

Avis, Paul. *Anglican Orders and the Priesting of Women*. London: Darton, Longman & Todd, 1999.

Avis, Paul, ed. *Seeking the Truth of Change in the Church: Reception, Communion and the Ordination of Women*. London: T & T Clark, 2003.

Baker, John Austin. *The Right Time*. London: Movement for the Ordination of Women, 1981.

Baker, Jonathan, ed. *Consecrated Women? A Contribution to the Women Bishops Debate*. Norwich, NFK: Canterbury, 2004.

Balthasar, Hans Urs von. *The Office of Peter and the Structure of the Church*. San Francisco: Ignatius, 1986.

Bam, Brigalia. *What is Ordination Coming to? Report of a Consultation on the Ordination of Women Held in Cartigny, Geneva, Switzerland, 21st–26th September 1970*. Geneva: World Council of Churches, 1971.

Barber, Paul. "What is a Peculiar?" *The Ecclesiastical Law Journal* 3 (1989) 299.

Barker, Margaret. *The Great High Priest*. Edinburgh: T & T Clark, 2003.

———. *Temple Theology: An Introduction*. London: SPCK, 2004.

Baron-Cohen, Simon. *The Essential Difference: Men, Women and the Extreme Male Brain*. London: Allen Lane, 2003.

Barr, Liz, and Andrew Barr. *Jobs for the Boys? Women who became Priests*. London: Hodder & Stoughton, 2001.

Bartsch, Hans W., and Reginald H. Fuller, eds. *Kerygma and Myth: A Theological Debate*. Vol. 1. London: SPCK, 1964.

Bauckham, Richard. *Gospel Women: Studies of the Named Women in the Gospels*. Edinburgh: T & T Clark, 2002.

Behr-Sigel, Elisabeth. *The Ministry of Women in the Church*. Redondo Beach, CA: Oakwood, 1990.

Behr-Sigel, Elisabeth, and Kallistos Ware. *The Ordination of Women in the Orthodox Church*. Geneva: World Council of Churches, 2000.

Bennett, Joyce Mary. *Hasten Slowly*. 2nd ed. Chichester, SXW: Little London Associates, 1992.

Bilezikian, Gilbert. "Renouncing the Love of Power for the Power of Love." In *How I Changed My Mind About Women in Leadership*, edited by Alan F. Johnson. Grand Rapids: Zondervan, 2010.

Blomfield, F. Cruttwell. *Wonderful Order*. London: SPCK, 1995.

Bogle, Joanna. *Women and the Priesthood*. London: Vox, 1987.

Borg, Marcus, and John Dominic Crossan. *The First Paul: Reclaiming the Radical Visionary behind the Church's Conservative Icon*. London: SPCK, 2009.

Boswell, John. *Christianity, Social Tolerance, and Homosexuality: Gay People in Western Europe from the Beginning of the Christian era to the Fourteenth Century*. Chicago / London: University of Chicago Press, 1980.

———. *The Marriage of Likeness: Same-sex Unions in Pre-modern Europe*. London: HarperCollins, 1995 [1994].

Bouyer, Louis. *Eucharist: Theology and Spirituality of the Eucharistic Prayer*. Notre Dame, IN: Notre Dame University Press, 1968.

———. *Woman in the Church*. San Francisco: Ignatius, 1979.

Bradley, Ian C. *The Power of Sacrifice*. London: Darton, Longman & Todd, 1995.

Bray, Gerald. "Bishops, Presbyters, and Women." *The Theologian: The Internet Journal for Integrated Theology* 2002. http://www.theologian.org.uk/church/bishops_presbyters_women.html.

Brent, Allen. *Cultural Episcopacy and Ecumenism*. Leiden, NLD: EJ Brill, 1992.

Bridge, G. Richmond. *Women and the Apostolic Ministry?* Halifax, NS: The Convent Society, 1997.

Brierley, P. W. *The Mind of Anglicans: What Church of England Clergy and Laity think about a wide range of aspects of Church Life and Ministry*. London: Christian Research / Cost of Conscience, 2003.

Broadhurst, John, ed. *Quo Vadis? The State Churches of Northern Europe*. Leominster, HEF: Gracewing, 1996.

Brown, Raymond E. "Roles of Women in the Fourth Gospel." In *The Community of the Beloved Disciple*. Mahwah, NJ: Paulist, 1979.

Bultmannm, Rudolf. *Jesus and the Word*. New York: Scribners, 1934.

Burer, Michael, and Daniel B. Wallace. "Was Junia Really an Apostle? A Re-examination of Romans 16:7." *New Testament Studies* 47 (2001) 76–91.

Butler, S. "The Priest as Sacrament of Christ the Bridegroom." *Worship* 66 (1992) 498–517.

Byrne, Lavinia. *Woman at the Altar: The Ordination of Women in the Roman Catholic Church*. London: Mowbray, 1994.

Canham, Elizabeth. *Pilgrimage to Priesthood*. London: SPCK, 1983.

Cappon, Lester J., ed. *The Adams-Jefferson Letters*. Chapel Hill, NC: UNC Press, 1987.

Carter, Douglas. *Debating the Ordination of Women*. London: Church Literature Association, 1974.

Chrysostom, John. *Homily on the Epistle to the Romans*.

Clack, Beverly, ed. *Misogyny in the Western Philosophical Tradition: A Reader*. London: Macmillan, 1999.

Clark, Elizabeth A. *Women in the Early Church*. Message of the Fathers of the Church 13. Wilmington, DE: Glazier, 1992.

Clark, Gillian. *Women in Late Antiquity: Pagan and Christian Lifestyles*. Oxford: OUP, 1993.

Clark, Lorenne. "Women and Locke: Who Owns the Apples in the Garden of Eden?" In *The Sexism of Social and Political Theory: Women and Reproduction from Plato to Nietzsche*, edited by Lorenne Clark and Lynda Lang, 16–40. Toronto: Toronto UP, 1979.

Clark, Stephen B. *Man and Woman in Christ: An Examination of the Roles of Men and Women in the Light of Scripture and the Social Sciences*. Ann Arbor, MI: Servant, 1980.

Clarke, Mary Cowden. *The Girlhood of Shakespeare's Heroines*. London: Bickers & Son, 1880.

Clayton, A. C. *The Rig-Veda and Vedic Religion: With Readings from the Vedas*. London: Christian Literature Society for India, 1913.

Connelly, Joan Breton. *Portrait of a Priestess: Women and Ritual in Ancient Greece*. Princeton: Princeton UP, 2007.

Cornwall, Susannah. "Intersex & Ontology: A Response to the Church, Women Bishops and Provision." Manchester: Lincoln Theological Institute, 2012.

Craston, Colin. *Biblical Headship and the Ordination of Women*. Bramcote, NTT: Grove, 1986.

Craston, Colin, et al. *Evangelicals and the Ordination of Women*. Bramcote, NTT: Grove, 1973.

Cross, F. L., and Elizabeth A. Livingstone, eds. *Oxford Dictionary of the Christian Church*. 3rd ed. Oxford: OUP, 1997.

Cumont, Franz Marie. *The Mysteries of Mithra*. Reprint, Charleston, SC: Bibliobazar, 1903.

Danby, Herbert, ed. *The Mishnah*. Oxford: OUP, 1933.

Danielou, Jean. *The Ministry of Women in the Early Church*. London: Faith, 1961.

Davies, W. D. *Paul and Rabbinic Judaism*. London: SPCK, 1958.

Delahaye, Karl. *Ecclesia Mater chez les Pères des trois premiers Siècles*. Paris: Éditions du Cerf, 1964.

De-la-Noy, Michael. *The Church of England: A Portrait*. London: Simon & Schuster, 1993.

Demant, Vigo Auguste. *Why the Christian Priesthood is Male*. 2nd ed. London: Church Literature Association, 1977.

Denny, Edward, and T. A. Lacey. *De Hierarchia Anglicana*. London: CJ Clay, 1895.

Dicken, Hélène. *Women and the Apostolic Ministry*. London: Church Literature Association, 1978.

Doe, Norman. *The Legal Framework of the Church of England: A Critical Study in a Comparative Context*. Oxford: Clarendon, 1996.

Donovan, Mary S. *Women Priests in the Episcopal Church: The Experience of the First Decade*. Cincinnati, OH: Forward Movement, 1988.

Dowell, Susan, and Jane Welch Williams. *Bread, Wine & Women: The Ordination Debate in the Church of England*. London: Virago, 1994.

Draper, Jonathan, ed. *Communion and Episcopacy: Essays to mark the Centenary of the Chicago-Lambeth Quadrilateral*. Oxford: Ripon College Cuddesdon, 1988.

Edwards, Ruth B. *The Case for Women's Ministry*. London: SPCK, 1989.

———. *Christian Priesthood*. 2nd ed. Edinburgh: Movement for Whole Ministry in the Scottish Episcopal Church, 1992.

BIBLIOGRAPHY

Eisen, Ute E. *Women Officeholders in Early Christianity: Epigraphical and Literary Studies.* Wilmington, DE: Michael Glazier, 2000.

Elwes, Teresa, ed. *Women's Voices: Essays in Contemporary Feminist Theology.* London: Marshall Pickering, 1992.

Epp, Eldon Jay. *Junia: The First Woman Apostle.* Minneapolis: Fortress, 2005.

————. "Text-critical, Exegetical, and Socio-cultural Factors Affecting the Junia/Junias Variation in Romans 16:7." In *New Testament Criticism and Exegesis: Festschrift J. Delobel,* edited by Joël Delobel and Adelbert Denaux, 227–92. Leuven, BEL / Sterling, VA: Peeters 2002.

Eusebius Pamphilius. *Ecclesiastical History.*

Farrer, Austin M. *The Glass of Vision.* London: Dacre, 1948.

Feuillet, André. *Le Cantique des Cantiques: Étude de Théologie Biblique et Réflexions sur une Méthode d'Exégèse.* Paris: Éditions du Cerf, 1953.

Field, Barbara. *Fit for This Office: Women and Ordination.* Melbourne: Collins Dove, 1989.

Fiorenza, Elisabeth Schüssler. *In Memory of Her: A Feminist Theological Reconstruction of Christian Origins.* London: SCM, 1983.

Fiorenza, Elisabeth Schüssler, and Hermann Häring. *The Non-Ordination of Women and the Politics of Power.* London: SCM, 1999.

Flaubert, Gustave. *A Sentimental Education.* Translated by Douglas Parmée. Oxford: Oxford Paperbacks, 2003.

France, R. T. *Women in the Church's Ministry: A Test-Case for Biblical Hermeneutics.* Carlisle, UK: Paternoster, 1995.

Francis, Leslie J., and Mandy Robbins. *The Long Diaconate, 1987–1994: Women Deacons and the Delayed Journey to Priesthood.* Leominster, HEF: Gracewing, 1999.

Franklin, Margaret Ann, ed. *The Force of the Feminine: Women, Men and the Church.* Sydney / London: Allen & Unwin, 1986.

Franklin, Margaret Ann, and Ruth Sturmey Jones, eds. *Opening the Cage: Stories of Church and Gender.* Sydney / London: Allen & Unwin, 1987.

Franklin, R. William, ed. *Anglican Orders: Essays on the Centenary of Apostolicæ Curae 1896–1996.* London: Mowbray, 1996.

Furlong, Monica. *Act of Synod—Act of Folly?* London: SCM, 1998.

————. *A Dangerous Delight: Women and Power in the Church.* London: SPCK, 1991.

————. *Feminine in the Church.* London: SPCK, 1984.

Gilchrist, Michael. *The Destabilisation of the Anglican Church: Women Priests and the Feminist Campaign to Replace Christianity.* North Melbourne, VIC: AD2000, 1991.

Gill, Sean. *Women and the Church of England from the Eighteenth Century to the Present.* London: SPCK, 1994.

Gimbutas, Marija. *The Language of the Goddess: Unearthing the Hidden Symbols of Western Civilization.* San Francisco: Harper & Row, 1989.

Goldberg, Steven. *The Inevitability of Patriarchy.* London: Temple Smith, 1977.

Gouges, Olympe de. "Declaration of the Rights of Woman and of the Female Citizen." In *The Portable Enlightenment Reader,* edited by Isaac Krammick, 609–17. New York: Penguin, 1995.

Grabar, André. *Christian Iconography: A Study of its Origins.* London: Routledge & Kegan Paul, 1969.

Grieger, Vernon S. *Earthly Images of the Heavenly Bride: Women and the Church.* Doncaster, VIC: Luther Rose, 1988.

Gumbley, K. F. W. "Church Legislation in the Isle of Man." *The Ecclesiastical Law Journal* 3 (2003) 240.

Guthrie, Harvey H., et al. *The Ordination of Women: An Exchange.* Atlanta: Catacomb Cassettes, 1970.

Habgood, John. "Thoughts on GRAS." *New Directions* 7 (2004).

Hailsham of St. Marylebone, Lord, ed. *Halsbury's Laws of England.* 4th edition. London: Butterworths, 1973.

Hampson, Margaret Daphne. *Theology and Feminism.* Oxford: Blackwell, 1990.

Harnack, Adolf von. *Ueber die beiden Recensionen der Geschichte der Prisca und des Aquila in Act. Apost. 18:1–27.* Berlin: Königl. Akad. der Wiss., 1900.

Harper, Michael. *Equal and Different.* London: Hodder & Stoughton, 1994.

Harris, Barbara C., et al. *Women's Ordination in the Episcopal Church Twenty-Five Years Later.* Cambridge, MA: Episcopal Divinity School, 2000.

Harvey, Andrew, and Anne Baring. *The Divine Feminine: Exploring the Feminine Face of God throughout the World.* Berkeley, CA: Conari, 1996

Haskins, Susan. *Mary Magdalen: Myth and Metaphor.* London: Harper Collins, 1993.

Hauke, Manfred. *Women in the Priesthood? A Systematic Analysis in the Light of the Order of Creation and Redemption.* San Francisco: Ignatius, 1988.

Hayter, Mary. *The New Eve in Christ the Use and Abuse of the Bible in the Debate About Women in the Church.* Grand Rapids: Eerdmans, 1987.

Hennecke, Edgar. *New Testament Apocrypha.* London: Lutterworth, 1965.

Henson, H. Hensley. "The Ordination of Women." In *Bishoprick Papers.* London: Oxford University Press, 1946.

Heyward, Carter. *A Priest Forever: One Woman's Controversial Ordination in the Episcopal Church.* Cleveland, OH: Pilgrim, 1999.

Hill, Christopher, and Edward Yarnold, eds. *Anglicans and Roman Catholics: The Search for Unity.* London: SPCK, 1994.

Hill, Mark. *Ecclesiastical Law.* 2nd ed. Oxford: OUP, 2001.

Hodgson, Leonard. *Theological Objections to the Admission of Women to Holy Orders.* London: Anglican Group for the Ordination of Women, 1967.

Holloway, Richard, ed. *Who Needs Feminism? Men Respond to Sexism in the Church.* London: SPCK, 1991.

Hook, Norman. *A Command of the Lord: The Theological Implications of Women in the Priesthood.* 2nd ed. London: Church Literature Association, 1977.

Hooker, Richard. *Of the Laws of Ecclesiastical Polity.* London: Dent, 1903.

Hope, David. "Sermon Preached at St. Bartholomew's, Armley on 3rd March 2004." *New Directions* 7 (2004).

Hopko, Thomas, ed. *Women and the Priesthood.* New York: St. Vladimir's Seminary, 1983.

Hume, David. *Essays and Treatises.* Oxford: OUP, 1962.

Hunwicke, John. "Pope Philogynes." *New Directions* 5 (2002).

Jardine, Lisa. *Still Harping on Daughters.* London: Harvester, 1983.

Johnson, Alan F., ed. *How I Changed My Mind About Women in Leadership.* Grand Rapids: Zondervan, 2010.

Jones, Ian. *Women and Priesthood in the Church of England: Ten Years On.* London: Church House, 2004.

Kassian, Mary A. *The Feminist Gospel.* Wheaton, IL: Crossway, 1992.

Kelly, J. N. D. *The Oxford Dictionary of Popes.* Oxford: OUP, 1986.

Kimel, Alvin F., ed. *Speaking the Christian God: The Holy Trinity and the Challenge of Feminism*. Grand Rapids: Eerdmanns, 1992.

Kirk, Geoffrey. "A Pertinent Preposition." *New Directions* 6 (2003).

Klein, Gunter. *The Twelve Apostles*. Göttingen, DEU: Vandenhoek & Ruprecht, 1961.

Knox, W. L. *St. Paul and the Church of the Gentiles*. Cambridge: CUP, 1939.

Leahy, Breandán. *The Marian Profile in the Ecclesiology of Hans Urs von Balthasar*. London: New City, 2000.

Leeder, Lynne. *Ecclesiastical Law Handbook*. London: Sweet & Maxwell, 1997.

Lerner, Gerda. *The Creation of Patriarchy*. New York: OUP, 1986.

Lewis, C. S. "Priestesses in the Church?" Originally published as "Notes on the Way." *Time and Tide* 29 (1948).

———. *The Screwtape Letters*. London: Fount, 1998.

———. *Undeceptions: Essays on Theology and Ethics*. London: Geoffrey Bles, 1971.

Locke, John. *First Treatise on Government*.

Lorber, Judith. "Dismantling Noah's Ark." In *Gender and Intimate Relationships: A Microstructural Approach*, edited by Barbara J. Risman and Pepper Schwartz, 89–101. Belmont, CA: Wadsworth, 1989.

Low, Robbie. "The Mind of Anglicans." *New Directions* 5 (2002).

Lubac, Henri de. *Les Églises Particulières dans l'Eglise Universelle*. Paris: Aubier, 1971.

———. *The Motherhood of the Church*. San Francisco: Ignatius, 1982.

———. *The Splendour of the Church*. London / New York: Sheed & Ward, 1956.

Macquarrie, John. *Theology, Church, and Ministry*. London: SCM, 1986.

Macy, Gary. *The Hidden History of Women's Ordination: Female Clergy in the Medieval West*. Oxford / New York: OUP, 2007.

Madigan, Kevin, and Carolyn Osiek, eds. *Ordained Women in the Early Church: A Documentary History*. Baltimore: John Hopkins Univ. Press, 2005.

Maitland, Sara. *A Map of the New Country Women and Christianity*. London: Routledge & Kegan Paul, 1983.

Mancinelli, Fabrizio. *The Catacombs of Rome and the Origins of Christianity*. Rome: Scala, 1981.

Mandeville, Bernard. *The Virgin Unmask'd*. London: G. Strahan, 1724.

Marshall, Rob. *Never the Same Again: A Journey Through Women's Ordination with the Bishop of London*. London: Darton, Longman & Todd, 1993.

Martimort, Aimé Georges. *Deaconesses: An Historical Study*. San Francisco: Ignatius, 1986.

Mascall, E. L. *Women Priests?* London: Church Literature Association, 1972.

Mason, Kenneth. *Mothers in God: A Catholic Perspective on Women as Bishops*. Edinburgh: Movement for Whole Ministry in the Scottish Episcopal Church, 1998.

McAddo, H. R. *Anglicans and Tradition and the Ordination of Women*. Norwich, NFK: Canterbury, 1997.

McGovern, Thomas J. *Priestly Identity: A Study in the Theology of Priesthood*. Dublin: Four Courts, 2001.

McLoughlin, William, and Jill Pinnock, eds. *Mary is for Everyone: Essays on Mary and Ecumenism*. Leominster, HEF: Gracewing, 1997.

Mitchell, Joseph R., and Helen B. Mitchell, eds. *Taking Sides: Clashing Views on Controversial Issues in Word Civilizations*. New York: McGraw-Hill, 1999.

Moll, Helmut, ed. *Church and Women: A Compendium*. San Francisco: Ignatius, 1988.

BIBLIOGRAPHY

Montefiore, Hugh. *Yes to Women Priests.* Great Wakering, ESS: Mayhew-McCrimmon / Oxford: Mowbray, 1978.

Moore, Paul. *Take a Bishop Like Me.* New York: Harper & Row, 1979.

Moore, Peter, ed. *Bishops: But What Kind? Reflections on Episcopacy.* London: SPCK, 1982.

———, ed. *Man Woman and Priesthood.* London: SPCK, 1978.

Morris, Joan. *Against Nature and God : The History of Women with Clerical Ordination and the Jurisdiction of Bishops.* London / Oxford: Mowbrays, 1973.

Morris, Leon, et al. *A Woman's Place [Documents of the Doctrine Commission of the General Synod of the Church of England in Australia].* Sydney: Anglican Information Office, 1976.

Müller, Gerhard. *Priesthood and Diaconate.* San Francisco: Ignatius, 2000.

Nairne, Penny. *Women Priests: Which Way Will You Vote?* London: SPCK, 1990.

Neave, Rosemary. *The Journey and the Vision: A Report on Ordained Anglican Women in the Church of the Province of New Zealand.* Newmarket, NZ: Women's Resource Centre, 1990.

Nichols, Aidan. *Holy Order: The Apostolic Ministry from the New Testament to the Second Vatican Council.* Dublin: Veritas, 1990.

Norman, Edward. *Church and Society in England 1770-1970: A Historical Study.* Oxford: OUP, 1976.

———. "Ecclesiastical Law Society Lecture: 'Authority in the Anglican Communion.'" *The Ecclesiastical Law Journal* 5 (2006) 172.

Norris, Richard A. "The Ordination of Women and the 'Maleness' of Christ." In *Feminine in the Church,* edited by Monica Furlong, 71–85. London: SPCK, 1984.

Norwich, John Julius. *The Popes: A History.* London: Chatto & Windus, 2011.

Ober, Leo. *Die Translation der Bischöfe im Altertum.* Archiv für Katholische Kirchenrecht 88. Mainz, DEU: Kirchheim, 1908.

Ochshorn, Judith. *The Female Experience and the Nature of the Divine.* Bloomington, IN: Indiana University Press, 1981.

Oddie, William. *What Will Happen to God? Feminism and the Reconstruction of Christian Belief.* London: SPCK, 1984.

Okure, Teresa. "The Significance Today of Jesus' Commission to Mary Magdalen," *International Review of Mission* 81 (1992) 177–88.

Origen of Alexandria. *Contra Celsum.* Book 4.

Otranto, G. "Note sul Sacerdozio Femminile nell'Antichita in Margine a una Testimonianza di Gelasio I." *Vetera Christianorum* 19 (1982) 48–76.

Pagden, Anthony. *The Enlightenment: And Why it still Matters.* Oxford: OUP, 2013.

Pagels, Elaine. "Visions, Appearances, and Apostolic Authority: Gnostic and Orthodox Traditions." In *Gnosis: Festschrift für Hans Jonas,* edited by Barbara Aland, 424–61. Göttingen, DEU: Vandenheok & Ruprecht, 1978.

Payne, Philip B. *Man and Woman: One in Christ; An Exegetical and Theological Study of Paul's Letters.* Grand Rapids: Zondervan, 2009.

Petre, Jonathan. *By Sex Divided: The Church of England and Women Priests.* London: Fount, 1994.

Piper, John, and Wayne Grudem, eds. *Recovering Biblical Manhood and Womanhood: A Response to Evangelical Feminism.* Wheaton, IL: Crossway, 1991.

Plaskow, Judith. "Christian Feminism and Anti-Judaism," *Cross Currents* 33 (1978) 307.

Podmore, Colin. *Aspects of Anglican Identity.* London: Church House, 2005.

Podmore, Colin, ed. *Community, Unity, Communion: Essays in Honour of Mary Tanner.* London: Church House, 1998.

Porter, Muriel. *Women in the Church: The Great Ordination Debate in Australia.* Ringwood, VIC / New York: Penguin, 1989.

Porter, Roy. *Flesh in the Age of Reason.* London: Allen Lane, 2003.

Puente, Pablo. "Letter of 6th November to Andrew Burnham." *New Directions* 6 (2002).

Quick, Oliver Chase. *The Christian Sacraments.* London: Nisbet, 1927.

Ratzinger, Joseph. *Called to Communion: Understanding the Church Today.* San Francisco: Ignatius, 1996.

————. *Principles of Catholic Theology: Building Stones for a Fundamental Theology.* San Francisco: Ignatius, 1987.

Rhoads, Steven E. *Taking Sex Differences Seriously.* San Francisco: Encounter, 2004.

Robinson, John A. T. *The Body: A Study in Pauline Theology.* London: SCM, 1952.

Robinson, James M., ed. *The Nag Hammadi Library in English.* New York: Harper Collins, 1990 [1988]. [First published, Leiden, NLD: E. J. Brill, 1977.]

Ruether, Rosemary Radford. *Full Incorporation of Women Into the Ministry of the Church.* Mahwah, NJ: Paulist, 1988.

————. *Women and Roman Catholic Christianity.* Washington, DC: Catholics for a Free Choice, 2000.

Rutler, George W. *Priest and Priestess.* Rosemont, PA: Good Shepherd, 2003.

Sanders, E. P. *The Historical Figure of Jesus.* London: Penguin, 1993.

Saward, John. *The Case Against the Ordination of Women.* 3rd rev. ed. London: Church Literature Association, 1978.

————. *Christ and His Bride: The Ordination of Women.* London: Church Literature Association, 1977.

Schiess, Betty Bone. *Why Me, Lord? One Woman's Ordination to the Priesthood with Commentary and Complaint.* New York: Syracuse University Press, 2003.

Schönborn, Christoph von. *God's Human Face: The Christ Icon.* San Francisco: Ignatius, 1994.

Schulz, S. "Transmigration und Translation: Studien zum Bischofswechsel." In *Der Spätantike bis zum Hohen Mittelalter.* Cologne, DEU: Böhlau, 1992.

Schweitzer, Albert. *The Quest of the Historical Jesus.* London: Adam & Charles Black, 1911.

Schweitzer, Albert, and William Montgomery. *The Mysticism of Paul the Apostle.* 2nd ed. Edinburgh: Adam & Charles Black, 1953 [1931].

Schweizer, Eduard. *Der Brief an Die Kolosser.* Zurich: Benzinger, 1976.

Shakespeare, William. *Troilus and Cressida.*

Shortt, Rupert. *Rowan's Rule: The Biography of the Archbishop.* London: Hodder & Stoughton, 2008.

Shouyi, Bai, and Chao Yang, eds. *An Outline History of China.* Beijing: Foreign Languages, 1982.

Sjöö, Monica, and Barbara Mor. *The Great Cosmic Mother: Rediscovering the Religion of the Earth.* San Francisco: Harper & Row, 1987. Originally published as *The Ancient Religion of the Great Cosmic Mother of All.* Trondheim, NOR: Rainbow, 1981.

Slee, Nicola. "Parables and Women's Experience." *The Modern Churchman* 26 (1984) 20–31.

Smail, Thomas Allan. *Forgotten Father: Rediscovering the Heart of the Christian Gospel.* London: Hodder & Stoughton, 1987.

Stagg, Evelyn, and Frank Stagg. *Woman in the World of Jesus*. Philadelphia: Westminster, 1978.

Stanford, Peter. *The She-Pope: Quest for the Truth Behind the Mystery of Pope Joan*. London: Arrow, 1999.

Steichen, Donna. *Ungodly Rage: The Hidden Face of Catholic Feminism*. San Francisco: Ignatius, 1991.

Stevenson, Kenneth. *Covenant of Grace Renewed*. London: Darton, Longman & Todd, 1994.

Stewart, H. F., trans. *Saepius Officio*. London: Church Literature Association, 1977.

Sykes, Stephen. *Unashamed Anglicanism*. London: Darton, Longman & Todd, 1995.

Tanner, Mary. "The Anglican Position on Apostolic Continuity and Apostolic Succession in the Porvoo Common Statement." In *Visible Unity and the Ministry of Oversight: The Second Theological Conference*. London: Church House, 1997.

Tertullian, Quintus. *Apologeticum*.

Thorne, Helen. *Journey to Priesthood: An in-depth Study of the First Women Priests in the Church of England*. Bristol: Centre for Comparative Studies in Religion and Gender, University of Bristol, 2000.

Thrall, Margaret E. *The Ordination of Women to the Priesthood*. London: SCM, 1958.

Tilby, Angela. *Everyman: The Hidden Tradition*. BBC broadcast Nov 8, 1992.

Tolhurst, James, ed. *Man, Woman and Priesthood*. Leominster, HEF: Gracewing, 1989.

Toon, Peter. *Let Wo[Men] Be Wo[Men]: Equality, Ministry and Ordination*. Leominster, HEF: Gracewing, 1990.

Torjesen, Karen Jo. *When Women Were Priests: Women's Leadership in the Early Church and the Scandal of Their Subordination in the Rise of Christianity*. New York: Harper Collins, 1993.

Torrance, Thomas F. *The Ministry of Women*. Edinburgh: Handsel, 1992.

———. "The Ministry of Women: An Argument for the Ordination of Women." *Touchstone* 5 (Fall 1992).

Vermes, Geza. *Searching for the Real Jesus: Jesus, the Dead Sea Scrolls and other Religious Themes*. London: SCM, 2009.

Wakeman, Hilary. *Women Priests the First Years*. London: Darton, Longman & Todd, 1996.

Waldron, Jeremy. *God, Locke and Equality: Christian Foundations in Locke's Political Thought*. Cambridge: CUP, 2002.

Walrond-Skinner, Sue. *Crossing the Boundary: What Will Women Priests Mean?* London: Mowbray, 1994.

Watts, Michael, ed. *Through a Glass Darkly: A Crisis Considered*. Leominster, HEF: Gracewing, 1993.

Webber, Andrew Lloyd, music, and lyrics by Tim Rice. *Jesus Christ Superstar*. London / New York: Leeds Music, 1970.

Webster, Margaret. *A New Strength, A New Song: The Journey to Women's Priesthood*. London: Mowbray, 1994.

Weinandy, Thomas G. *Does God Change? The Word's becoming in the Incarnation*. Still River, MA: St. Bede's, 1985.

Wetherell, David. *Women Priests in Australia? The Anglican Crisis*. Melbourne: Spectrum, 1987.

Wickham, Chris. *The Inheritance of Rome: A History of Europe from 400 to 1000*. London: Penguin, 2009.

Wijngaards, J. N. M. *Did Christ Rule Out Women Priests?* Great Wakering, ESS: McCrimmon's, 1986.

———. *No Women in Holy Orders?* Norwich, NFK: Canterbury, 2002.

———. *The Ordination of Women in the Catholic Church: Unmasking a Cuckoo's Egg Tradition.* London: Darton, Longman & Todd, 2001.

Williams, Rowan. "The Structures of Unity." *New Directions* 6 (2003).

Wilson, Harold. *Women Priests? Yes, Now!* Nutfield, SRY: Denholm House, 1975.

Wilson, W. Gilbert. *Why No Women Priests?* Worthing, SXW: Churchman, 1988.

Winter, Miriam Therese. *The Gospel According to Mary: A New Testament for Women.* New York: Orbis, 2008.

Wright, N. T. *The Resurrection of the Son of God.* Minneapolis: Fortress, 2003.

———. "A Return to Christian Origins (Again)." *Bible Review* 15 (1999) 10–12.

Young, Frances M. *Presbyterial Ministry in the Catholic Tradition, or, Why Shouldn't Women Be Priests?* Exeter, DEV: Methodist Sacramental Fellowship, 1994.

Zamoyski, Adam. *Phantom Terror: The Threat of Revolution and the Repression of Liberty 1789–1848.* London: William Collins, 2014.

Zizioulas, John D. *Being as Communion.* New York: St. Vladimir's Seminary, 1997.

———. *Eucharist, Bishop, Church: The Unity of the Church in the Divine Eucharist and the Bishop during the First Three Centuries.* Brookline, MA: Holy Cross Orthodox, 2001.

Other Sources

Advisory Council for the Church's Ministry / Council for Women's Ministry in the Church. *Women in Ministry: A Study.* London: Church Information Office, 1968.

Anglican Consultative Council. *The Time is Now: Report of the ACC Meeting at Limuru, Kenya, 23 February—5 March 1971.* London: SPCK, 1971.

Anglican Mission in America. *Report of the Study Concerning the Ordination of Women.* Pawleys Island, SC: AMiA, 2003.

Anglican-Methodist Commission on Women and Holy Orders. *Women and the Ordained Ministry Report of an Anglican-Methodist Commission on Women and Holy Orders.* London: SPCK / Epworth, 1968.

Anglican-Roman Catholic International Commission. *ARCIC I Final Report.* London: CTS/SPCK, 1982.

———. *The Gift of Authority: Authority in the Church III.* London: Catholic Truth Society, 1999.

Archbishops' Commission on Christian Doctrine. *Doctrine in the Church of England.* London: SPCK, 1938.

Catholic Church. *Catechism of the Catholic Church.* Dublin: Veritas, 1994.

———. *The Code of Canon Law (in English Translation).* London: Harper Collins, 1983.

———. *The Rites of the Catholic Church as Revised by Decree of the Second Vatican Council and Published by Authority of Pope Paul VI.* New York: Pueblo, 1976–80.

Central Advisory Council on Training and Ministry. *Gender and Ministry.* London: Church Information Office, 1962.

Church of England. *The Canons of the Church of England.* 6th ed. London: Church House, 2000.

———. *Church of England Year Book 2004.* London: Church House, 2004.

Commission appointed by the Archbishops of Canterbury and York. *Women and Holy Orders*. London: Church Information Office, 1966.

Committee appointed by His Grace the Archbishop of Canterbury. *The Ministry of Women*. London: SPCK, 1919.

Eames Commission. *The Archbishop of Canterbury's Commission on Communion and Women in the Episcopate: The Official Reports*. Toronto: Anglican Book Centre, 1994.

Faith and Order Board, Scottish Episcopal Church. *Green Paper—A Paper for Discussion within the Scottish Episcopal Church*. Edinburgh: Scottish Episcopal Church, 2001.

Forward in Faith. *Agreed Statement on Communion*. London: FiF, 1993.

General Synod. *The Ordination of Women to the Priesthood: The Synod Debate 11 November 1992* [The Verbatim Record]. London: Church House, 1993.

General Synod. "February [2014] Group of Sessions." *Report of Proceedings* 45 (2014).

General Synod Working Group on Women in the Episcopate. *Episcopal Ministry and Women: A Draft Issues Paper*. Sydney, NSW: Anglican Church of Australia, 2003.

Inter Orthodox Consultation on the Place of the Woman in the Orthodox Church and the Question of the Ordination of Women. *Conclusions of the Inter Orthodox Consultation on the Place of the Woman in the Orthodox Church and the Question of the Ordination of Women (Rhodes, Greece, 30 Oct.—7 Nov. 1988)*. Minneapolis: Light & Life, 1990.

Roman Catholic Sources

John Paul II. *Christifideles Laici*. London: Catholic Truth Society, 1989.

———. *Familiaris Consortio*. Vatican City: Vatican Council Documents, 1981.

———. *Mulieris Dignitatem, Apostolic Letter on the Dignity and Vocation of Women*. London: Catholic Truth Society, 1988.

———. "Ordinatio Sacerdotalis." *Acta Apostolicae Sedis* 86 (1994) 545–48.

Leo XIII. *Apostolicae Curae*. London: Catholic Truth Society, 1887.

Paul VI. *Gaudium et Spes*. Vatican City: Vatican Council Documents, 1965.

Sacred Congregation for the Doctrine of the Faith. *Inter Insigniores (Declaration on the Question of Admission of Women to the Ministerial Priesthood)*. Vatican City, 1976.

———. *Letter to the Bishops of the Catholic Church on the Collaboration of Men and Women in the Church and in the World*. Vatican City, 2004.

———. *The Ordination of Women Official Commentary from the Sacred Congregation for the Doctrine of the Faith on its Declaration Inter Insigniores of 15th October 1976*. London: Catholic Truth Society, 1977.

Vatican II. *Dogmatic Constitution on the Church [Lumen Gentium]*. Boston, MA: Pauline, 1964.

Other

World Council of Churches. *Baptism, Eucharist and Ministry*. Geneva: World Council of Churches, 1982.

———. *Concerning the Ordination of Women: A Symposium*. Geneva: World Council of Churches, 1964.

General Synod Documents

GS 104. *The Ordination of Women to the Priesthood.* London: Church Information Office, 1972.*

GS 252. *The Ordination of Women: Report of the Standing Committee on the Reference to the Dioceses.* London: Church Information Office, 1973.

GS Misc 88. *Ordination of Women: A Supplement to the Consultative Document GS 104 (Prepared at the request of the Standing Committee by Miss Christian Howard).* London: Church Information Office, 1978.*

GS Misc 198. *Ordination of Women to the Priesthood: Further Report; A Background Paper by Christian Howard. London: Church Information Office, 1984.*

GS 694. *The Priesthood of the Ordained Ministry.* London: General Synod Board for Mission and Unity, 1986.

GS 738. *The Ordination of Women to the Priesthood: The Scope of the Legislation.* London: General Synod of the Church of England, 1986.

GS Misc 246. *The Ordination of Women to the Priesthood: The Scope of the Legislation (GS 738); Memorandum by the House of Bishops.* London: General Synod of the Church of England, 1986.

GS 764. *The Ordination of Women to the Priesthood: First Report by the House of Bishops.* London: General Synod of the Church of England, 1987.

GS 829. *The Ordination of Women to the Priesthood: A Second Report by the House of Bishops.* London: General Synod of the Church of England, 1988.

GS 944. *Episcopal Ministry [The Cameron Report].* London: Church House, 1990.

GS 996. *The Ordination of Women to the Priesthood: Reference of the Legislation to the Dioceses; Voting Figures.* London: General Synod of the Church of England, 1992.

GS 830Y. *Draft Priests (Ordination of Women) Measure: Draft Canon C4B and Draft Amending Canon No. 13; Revision Committee Report.* London: General Synod of the Church of England, 1992.

GS 1019. *Senior Church Appointments: A Review of the Methods of Appointment of Area and Suffragan Bishops, Deans, Provosts, Archdeacons and Residentiary Canons.* London: Church House, 1992.

GS 1202. *Anglican-Moravian Conversations.* London: Council for Christian Unity, 1996.

GS 1248. *Eucharistic Presidency: A Theological Statement by the House of Bishops of the Church of England.* London: Church House, 1997.

GS Misc 580. *Bishops in Communion: Collegiality in the Service of the Koinonia of the Church.* London: Church House, 2000.

GS 1395. *Episcopal Ministry Act of Synod: Report of a Working Party of the House of Bishops [The Blackburn Report].* London: General Synod of the Church of England, 2000.

Bibliography

GS Misc 632. *The Eucharist: Sacrament of Unity: An Occasional Paper of the House of Bishops of the Church of England.* London: Church House, 2001.

GS 1457. *Working Party on Women in the Episcopate: A Progress Report from the House of Bishops.* London: General Synod of the Church of England, 2002.

GS 1557. *Women Bishops in the Church of England? A Report of the House of Bishops Working Party on Women in the Episcopate.* London: General Synod of the Church of England, 2004.

GS Misc 807. *Women Bishops in the Church of England? A Report of the House of Bishops Working Party on Women in the Episcopate: Ecumenical Responses.* London: General Synod of the Church of England, 2005.

GS 1605. *House of Bishops' Women Bishops Group: Report to the General Synod from a Working Group Chaired by the Bishop of Guildford.* London: General Synod of the Church of England, 2006.

GS Misc 826. *Women in the Episcopate: Report to the House of Bishops from the Bishops of Guildford and Gloucester.* London: General Synod of the Church of England, 2006.

GS 1685. *Women Bishops: Report of the Women Bishops Legislative Drafting Group.* London: General Synod of the Church of England, 2008.

*These reports were the work of Dame Christian Howard.

Subject Index

adam, 121
Adam of Usk, 106
Adie, Michael, 116–21, 124, 127, 128,
    130, 131, 134
Advisory Council for the Church's
    Ministry, xi
Aesop, 63
Agnes. *See* Pope Joan
Ambrose, 91
Andronicus, 42, 67, 68–69, 71
Anglican Consultative Council, xi
Anglicanism. *See also* Church of England
    dogma of, 119
    nature of, 116
Apollinarius, 127
Apollos, 69
apostles, role of, 86–88
Apostles, the (the Twelve)
    choice of, 42, 43
    Jewishness of, 43
    and the kingdom of God, 43
    maleness of, 43
    women ministering to, 41–42
apostola Apostolorum, 81, 86, 88
apostolate, choice of, 31
Aquila, 67
Aquinas, Thomas, 15, 19, 50, 83–84, 100
Aristotle, 15, 50
Armstrong, Karen, 90
Arnold, Matthew, 49

asceticism, 110
assembly, speaking in, 59, 60 , 61
Astell, Mary, 28, 30
Augustine of Hippo, 19, 50, 92

Barnabas, 88
Baron-Cohen, Simon, 21
Barth, Karl, 122
Bartholomew, Apostle, 92
Basilica of S. Pressede, 74, 75
Bauckham, Richard, 42, 70–71
Bayle, Pierre, 28
Beatitudes, 52
Belly and the Members, fable of, 63
Beloved Disciple, 78, 80
Bennett, Gary, xiii, xiv
Bethany, anointing at, 39–40
Bible
    androcentricity of, 113
    authority of, 130
    equality of the sexes, not addressed
        in, 124
    inclusive language in, 25–26, 41
    patriarchy of, 18–19
    social practices based on, 124
Bilezikian, Gilbert, 34
Blondel, David, 107
Boccaccio, Giovanni, 77
Borg, Marcus, 67
Boswell, James, 108–9

Bouyer, Louis, 100
Broadhurst, John, 133
Brown, Dan, 93, 111
Brunner, Emil, 122
Bultmann, Rudolf, 2, 3, 10, 79
Burer, Michael, 69–70
Byrne, Lavinia, 97, 102, 111

canonicity, xv, 3
Canterbury Tales (Chaucer), 27
Capella Graeca, 96, 97–102
Carey, George, 126, 131, 132, 135
Carolingian Empire, 104
Carravaggio, 82
Catacomb of Priscilla, 73, 76, 96–102, 114
Catacomb of SS Peter and Marcellinus,
        101
Catacomb of St. Callixtus, 73, 101–2
Catholic Church
        freeing Jesus from Jewish patriarchal
                context, 46
        tradition in, 114
Celsus, 56
Cerularius, Michael, 107–8
chaise percée, 107
Charlemagne, 103, 104
Charles of Anjou, 94
Chartism, 22
Chaucer, Geoffrey, 27
Christ, 2. See also Jesus
        cultural context for, 15
        representation of, 15, 130
        risen, 79–85
Christian church, as body of risen Christ,
        64
Christian feminists, 8
        conspiracy theories and, 88
        cultural imperialism of, 25
        on Jesus's sex, 12
        reconstructing early Christianities,
                20–22
        relationship of, with biblical and
                Christian past, 17–20
Christianity
        committed to miracles, 3–4
        Democracy and, 129
        dogmatic structure of, 4

as domestic church, 67
early forms of, 47, 56, 68–69
early functions in, 69
as historical religion, 1, 24, 47
particularity and, 1, 8
Paul as founder of, 50
reinterpretation of, 2–3
rejection of, 6, 8. 30
retrospective nature of, 19
socialism and, 22
translation and, 25
"Christianity and . . ." syndrome, 22
Chrysostom, John, 67, 68
Church of England. See also Anglicanism
        attendance figures for, 131–32
        challenges to, xv
        women's ordination in, xi–xiii,
                116–35
Church and the Second Sex, The (Daly),
        90
Church of S. Praxedis, 97, 102–5
Cicero, 50, 64
Clack, Beverley, 19
Clark, Elizabeth A., 109–10
Clark, Lorenne, 123
Clarke, Mary Cowden, 89
Cledonius, 127
Clovis, 104
Colosseum, 24
comprehensive theory, 53
concelebration, 24, 97–100
concretion, 8, 10, 12
Condorcet (Marie Jean Antoine Nicolas
        de Caritat), 58, 111–12
conspiracy theories, 17, 85, 87, 88,
        111–12
Constitution on the Church in the
        Modern World (Gaudium et Spes;
        Vatican II), 124
Coriolanus (Shakespeare), 62, 63
Cornwall, Susannah, 13–14
Cottrell, Stephen, 48–49, 50, 54, 64, 65
Council of Constance, 106
Council of Frankfurt, 103
"Council of Jerusalem," 54
creation accounts, 123
creation narratives, 44

creeds, xv
Crossan, John Dominic, 67
Cyril of Jerusalem, 91

D'Alembert, Jean, 20
Daly, Mary, 90
Dante, 46
Dark Ages, women's social role in, 104
Davies, W. D., 52
Da Vinci Code, The (Brown), 112
deacons
    female, 110
    role of, 98
Dead Sea Scrolls, 32, 90
Declaration of the Rights of Man and of
    the Citizen (August 26, 1789)
    (French National Constituent
    Assembly), 29
Declaration of the Rights of Woman, The
    (de Gouges), 29–30
De Gouges, Olympe, 29–30
Demant, V. A., xiii, 16
De Noblitatis et Rusticitata Dialogus
    (Haemerlein), 107
Descartes, Rene, 19
Diderot, Denis, 4, 19, 58, 111
dissimilarity, 32–33, 44
divine female, 109
divine law, 30
divorce, 43–44, 121
Dodd, C. H., 33
Dominicans, Mary Magdalen and, 94

ecclesiastical authority, 117
egalitarianism, 8, 19, 47
Eliezer, Rabbi (*Eliezer* ben Hyrcanus), 61
Enlightenment, 8, 19–20, 112
    achievements of, 49–50
    feminism's roots in, 28–29
Enquiry Concerning Human
    Understanding, An (Hume), 4–5
Epaenetus, 67
Epaphroditus, 69, 86, 88
Epiphanius of Salamis, 68, 89
Epp, Eldon, 69–70
Equicola, Mario, 107
eschatology, 33

Eucharist, depictions of, 24, 97, 98
eunuchs, 107–8
Eusebius, 35, 91
Everyman: The Hidden Tradition, 96–99
exorcism, 34, 36

Fall, the, 90, 122
familia Caesaris, 55, 56
Familiaris Consortio (John Paul II), 124
family, importance of, 35
Farrer, Austin, 9–10, 12, 86
Faull, Vivienne, 132, 134
feminism. *See also* Christian feminists
    Christianity and, 7
    Enlightenment and, 28–29
    first conscious stage of, 27
    goal of, 27–28
    rejection of, 8
Feuerbach, Ludwig, 124
Filmer, Robert, 28, 123
Flaubert, Gustave, 22
forgiveness, 40
"Fractio Panis," 73, 76, 99. *See also*
    Catacomb of Priscilla
Franciscans, 94
Freud, Sigmund, 124
fulfillment, personal, 46

Gaia and God (Reuther), 90
Garth, Helen, 78
gender inclusivity, 47
Gentiles, 51–54
Girlhood of Shakespeare's Heroines, The
    (Clarke), 89
Gnostic Gospels, The (Pagels), 90
Gnostic texts, 89–92
God, image of, 120–24
goddess, the, 109
Goldberg, Steven, 21
golden age, myth of, 91
Golden Ass, The, 55
Golden Lie (of Plato), 64
Gospel of Thomas, 90
Gospel according to Woman, The
    (Armstrong), 90
Grabar, André, 100–101
Graham, Alec, 118, 120, 125–26

Great Commission, 88
Gregory the Great, 39, 88, 92–93
Gregory Nazianzen, 126, 127–28
Grünewald, Matthias, 72, 78

Hadrian, 55
Haemerlein, Felix, 107
Haggard, Rider, 21
Hampson, Daphne, 1, 5–12, 16, 18–19,
    25, 30, 113–14
Handel, George Frideric, 51
Harnack, Adolf von, 67
Haskins, Susan, 78
healing, 34–35
Henson, Henley, xiii
heretical movements, 91
Herodotus, 86
Heyward, Carter, 16
Hidden Tradition, The, 109
Hilary of Poitiers, 92
Hinduism, 63
Hippolytus, 91
Historical Figure of Jesus, The (Sanders),
    78
*Historical Jesus, The: The Life of a
    Mediterranean Jewish Peasant,* 32
historical research, 32
Hitler, Adolf, 14
Hobbes, Thomas, 19, 28
Holy Blood and Holy Grail, The, 111
Home, Henry, 4
homosexual marriage, 132, 134
Hooker, Richard, xv, 116–18, 120, 126
hospitality, 34
Howard, Christian, xi–xii, 129
human rights, 49
Hume, David, 4–5, 19
Hus, Jan, 106

iconoclast controversy, 15, 107
iconography, paleo-Christian, 100–101
Ignatius of Antioch, 15
imago dei, 120–24
Incarnation, 12, 25, 45
inclusive language, 25–26, 41
Inevitability of Patriarchy (Goldberg), 21

In Memory of Her (Schussler-Fiorenza),
    90
Innocent VII, 106
Inter Insigniores (Sacred Congregation for
    the Doctrine of the Faith), 11
intersex, 13–14
Irenaeus of Lyons, 124
Islam, 25
Israel, reconstruction of, 43

Jairus, daughter of, 35
James, M. R., 92
Jansen, Katherine, 78
Jardine, Lisa, 17, 19
Jefferson, Thomas, 9
Jenkins, David, xiii, 4
Jenkins, Philip, 95
Jerome, 68
Jesus, 135
    anamnesis of, 16
    attitude of, toward women, 17–18,
        22–23, 27, 31, 46–47, 115
    characteristics of, and being the
        Christ, 46
    choosing male apostles, 31, 42, 43
    cultural context of, 32–33
    on divorce, 43–44, 121
    egalitarianism of, 23
    encounters of, with women, 33–40
    genderless, 13
    God revealed through, 1
    historical, 2–3, 6, 25, 31, 32–33, 47
    intersexed, 13–14
    Jewishness of, 2, 45
    linking of, to causes, 22
    maleness of, 11–13, 15, 127–28
    ministry of, 33, 51–52
    parables of, women in, 40–41
    portrayals of, 44–45
    preaching style of, 32–33
    relevance of, 46
    respecting the Torah, 34–35, 52
    teachings of, 42
    tomb of, 79–81
    truths about, 32
    women ministering to, 41–42
Jesus the Jew, 32

Jesus and Judaism, 32
Jesus Movement, 23, 33, 90
*Jesus of Nazareth, King of the Jews: A
    Jewish Life and the Emergence of
    Christianity,* 32
Jesus Seminar, 32–33
Jewish Law, 54
Joan. *See* Pope Joan
Joanna. See Junia/s
Joanna (wife of Chuza), 41–42, 80
John Paul II, 31, 124
Josephus, 37, 86
Josephus, Flavius, 32
Judaism
    internal conflicts of, 53
    prohibitions in, on women's speaking,
        61
Junia/s, 41, 67–71, 115

Kant, Immanuel, 19
kerygma, 9
King, Ursula, 90
kingdom of God, 33, 42–43, 51, 52–53,
        64
Klein, Gunter, 86–87
Knox, W. L., 52

Lady Theodora. *See* Theodora, Lady
La Fleche, Jesuits at, 4–5
Latimer Trust, 13
Lazarus, 39, 82
L'Education Sentimentale (Flaubert), 22
Leo III, 104
Leo IV, 104
Leo IX, 107
Leonard, Graham, 116
Lerner, Gerda, 27
Lessing, Gotthold Ephram, 2
Lewis, C. S., xiii, 9, 22, 131
Livy, 63
Lloyd-Webber, Andrew, 89
Locke, John, 5, 19, 28, 123–24, 129–30
Longley, Clifford, xii
Lorber, Judith, 27–28
Lothair, 104
Louis the Pious, 103, 104
Lunn, David, 133–35

Luther, Martin, 122

Macy, Gary, 110
Madigan, Kevin, 110
Magdalen Houses, 94
Magdalen Studies, 78, 95
Mailly, Jean de, 106
male priests, representing male savior,
        14–15
Malvern, Marjorie, 78
Mancinelli, Fabrizio, 101–2
Mandeville, Bernard, 28–29
*Marginal Jew, A: Rethinking the Historical
        Jesus,* 32
marriage
    divine love and, 11
    remarriage, 44
    same-sex, 132, 134
Martha of Bethany, 38–39, 91
Martin Polonus, 106, 107
Marx, Karl, 124
Mary (Mother of God), 74, 92–93, 105
Mary (mother of James and Joseph), 41,
        79, 80
Mary (sister of Martha), 38–39, 40
Mary Magdalen, 35, 41, 70, 115
    as apostle, 87
    as apostola Apostolorum, 81, 86
    Catholics' view of, 94
    as feminist icon, 79, 95
    in Gnostic texts, 91–92
    knowledge about, 78–81
    Luke's sinner and, 92–93, 94
    and Mary (Mother of God), 92–93
    portrayals of, 23–24
    Protestants' view of, 94
    relocation of, 93–94
    in resurrection appearances, 79–82
    significance of, 82–86
    stories surrounding, 89–94
*Mary Magdalen: Myth and Metaphor
        (Haskins),* 78
Mascall, Eric, xiii, 16
matriarchal societies, 20–21
Matthias, 86, 87
Mead, Margaret, 21

Merry Wives of Windsor, The
    (Shakespeare), 89
Mill, John Stuart, 21
miracles, 3–6
Mishnah, 37, 61
misogyny
    in the Bible, 6–7
    conspiracy regarding, 17
Misogyny in the Western Philosophical
    Tradition (Clack), 19
Mithraism, 55
Moore, Paul, 15–16
Morris, Joan, 24, 97, 102, 108
Movement for the Ordination of Women,
    13, 24
mulier tacet texts, 23
mystery religions, 55
mythos, 9

Nag Hammadi collection, 90
Nain, widow of, 35
natural law, 30
New Woman, New Earth (Reuther), 90
Nicephorus, 104
Norris, Richard A., Jr., 14–15, 34, 45,
    126–28

Ochshorn, Judith, 3
Oddie, William, 7
Oedipus, 12
Okure, Teresa, 82
one-substance doctrine, 5
Order of Preachers. *See* Dominicans
orders of the church, as gift of the Lord,
    xiv–xv
ordination, meaning of, 110
Origen, 68
orphans, 35
Osiek, Carolyn, 110

Pagden, Anthony, 19–20, 46
Pagels, Elaine, 87–88, 90
Paradise Lost (Milton), 46
Paradise Regained (Milton), 46
parousia, 53
particularity, 1
Paschal I, 24, 75, 97, 102, 103–5

Passion, 40
Patriarcha (Filmer), 28
patriarchy, 15, 112
    in the Bible, 6–7
    endurance of, 21
    fall into, 90, 110
Paul
    achievement of, 57
    as apostle, 87
    attitude of, toward slaves, 55–58
    authority of, 59–60
    eschatology of, 53–54, 64–65
    intentions of, 50–51
    internal conflicts of, 53, 54
    as inventor/founder of Christianity,
        50
    Jewishness of, 52
    obedience as doctrine of, 64
    as Pharisee, 52
    portrayals of, 23
    priorities of, 115
    on public worship, 58–61
    social conservatism of, 62
    theology of, 59, 62
    worldview of, 50–51
Paul VI, 11
Peter, 75, 80
Philemon, letter to, 56–57
Phoebe, 67, 68–69
Photius, 107
Pistis Sophia, 90
Plaskow, Judith, 45
Platina, Bartolomeo, 106
Plato, 15, 64
Plutarch, 63
Podmore, Colin, xi, xii
Pope Joan (Joanna), 24, 77, 97, 105–8,
    111, 116
Pope Joan (dir. Anderson), 108
Pope Joan board, 76
Porter, Roy, 49
post-Christian culture, 65
Praxedis, Saint, 105
Pressede, Saint, 75
priestesses, 109
Priestly, Joseph, 9
Prisca (Priscilla), 24, 67

Pudens, 105
Pudentia, Saint, 105

Quest for the Historical Jesus. See Jesus, historical

Ramsey, Michael, 62–63
Ratzinger, Joseph, 2
realized eschatology, 33
reason, 116–17
redemption, 15
Reformation, 91
reign of God. See kingdom of God
Reimarus, Hermann Samuel, 2, 47
religious toleration, 49–50
Renaissance, 91
repentance, 36
restoration eschatology, 43
Resurrection, 39
    belief in, 95
    Jesus's sex and, 13
resurrection appearances, 79–85, 87–88
Reuther, Rosemary Radford, 90
Revolution of 1688, 28
Rhoads, Steven, 21
Rice, Tim, 89
Rig-Veda, 63
Robespierre, Maximilien, 58
Robinson, John, 62–63
Roman catacombs, 24, 113
Rossi, Mary Ann, 98–99, 102
Rousseau, Jean Jacques, 19, 58, 111, 135
Rubens, Peter Paul, 72, 78
Runcie, Robert, xiii

Sabbath healings, 36
Salic Law, 104
Salome, 41, 79
salvation, 37, 53, 127
salvation history, 32, 45, 64
Samaritans, 36–37
Sanders, E. P., 35, 43, 52, 78
Saxer, Victor, 78
Schussler Fiorenza, Elisabeth, 70, 90, 113
Schweitzer, Albert, 2, 3, 25, 33, 45, 53–54, 56–57
scripture, 116–17, 120–25. See also Bible

as narrative, 11, 85
patriarchal and misogynist roots of, 6–7
study of, 5–6
women's ordination and, 118
Second Council of Nicaea, 25, 103
self-awareness, 46
Seventh Council. See Second Council of Nicaea
sexes, equality of, 7, 50, 123–24, 129–30, 134
sexual difference, common experience of, 12
sexual identity, as social construct, 14
Shakespeare, William, 17, 62, 89
She-Pope, The (Stanford) 109
Siena Cathedral, 75, 112–13
similarity, 32, 44
sinner, anointing by, 40
Sixtus IV, 106
Sketch for an Historical Picture of the Progress of the Human Mind (Concordet), 111–12
slavery
    in Pauline churches, 55–58
    in the Roman Empire, 55
slave trade, demise of, 50
Slee, Nicola, 19, 113
social hierarchy, 64
social structures, reflecting sex differences, 21
society, as a body, 63
Socrates, 14, 63
souls, classification of, 64
Spinoza, Baruch (Benedict), 5–9, 24–25, 28
Stagg, Evelyn, 34, 42, 45
Stagg, Frank, 34, 42, 45
Stanford, Peter, 105, 108, 109
St. Maximin monastery, 93–94
Subjection of Women, The (Mill), 21
suffragette movement, 129
Susanna, 41
syncretism, 37
synoptic Gospels, references in, to women, 34
Syrophoenician woman, 37–38, 51–52

systematic theology, 59

Tanner, Mary, xiv
television, bad history and, 109
Tertullian, 19, 54–55
The Deposition (Rubens), 72
The Isenheim Altarpiece (Grunewald), 72
Theodora, Lady, 74, 97, 102–5, 107, 111,
    114–15
Theodora Episcopa, 24
Theodore the Studite, 103
Theodulph of Orleans, 104
theology, images and, 10
Theology and Feminism (Hampson), 1,
    7–8
three-legged stool (of Hooker), 116–17,
    120
Tilby, Angela, 97, 99, 102
tongues, speaking in, 59, 60–61
Torah
    authority of, 53
    observance of, 34, 44, 52
Torjesen, Karen, 109
Torrance, Thomas F., 97–100, 102–5, 126
tradition, 116–17, 125–35
translation, 25
Trible, Phyllis, 113
Twelve, the, 86–87, 88, 115
Twelve Apostles, The (Klein), 86–87

Valentinians, 126
Vermes, Geza, 2
Virgin Unmask'd, The (Mandeville), 28
Voltaire, 4, 58
Voraigne, Jacobus de, 94

Waldron, Jeremy, 123
Wallace, Daniel B., 69–70
Warner, Marina, 91
Weber, Hans-Ruedi, 11–12
Weeping Magdalens, 95
Weiss, Johannes, 33
Welby, Justin, 135
Wesley, Charles, 13
Wesley, John, 13
West, Enlightenment narratives of, 49–50
What Will Happen to God? (Oddie), 7

Wickham, Chris, 104
widows, 35, 36
widow's mite, 36
Williams, Rowan, xiii–xiv, 7–8
Williamson, Roy, 132–33
Wilpert, Joseph, 99, 102, 111
Winter, Miriam, 91
woman bent double, 36, 40
woman taken in adultery, 36
woman at the well in Samaria, 36–37, 40
women
    as priests, evidence for, 24
    religious communities of, 38–39
    speaking in church, 58–61
    subordination of, 15
*Women in the Early Church: Message of
    the Fathers of the Church* (Clark),
    109–10
women's ordination, 3
    abstract approaches to, 45–46
    antipathy toward, 119
    attracting congregants through, 132
    in Catholic Church, 11, 114
    in the Church of England, xi–xiv,
        116–35
    claims for, 109
    conspiracy theories and, 111–12
    correcting religious imagery, 12,
        15–16
    discussion of, reluctance about, xiii
    in Episcopal Church in the USA, 11
    in Gnostic groups, 126
    Jesus's actions and, 45
    Jesus's apostles and, 31–32, 42
    as justice issue, 58, 119, 132
    Mary Magdalen and, 95
    scripture and, 118
    as second-order issue, 118, 131
    Spinoza's support for, 7
    universal suffrage and, 129
women's rights, 50, 128
Women and Spirituality (King), 90
World Council of Churches, Faith and
    Order Commission, xii
worship, public, 58–61
Wright, Tom, xiii, 79, 82, 84, 88–89, 95

Scripture Index

OLD TESTAMENT

Genesis

1:17	44
1:26	122
1:26–27	120
2:24	44
5:1–3	121
9:6	121

Leviticus

1:3	18
15:25–33	34
20:18	34

Deuteronomy

14:29	35
24:17	35

Isaiah

11:11f.	87
49:6	52
56:6–8	87

Hosea

1:2	18

Micah

2:12	87

Zechariah

2:11	87

NEW TESTAMENT

Matthew

5:31f.	44
5:31ff.	43
7:21–23	60
8:14–15	33
9:20–22	18
10:4	121
10:5–6	37
10:6	51
12:7	36
15:21–28	34
19:3–9	18, 43, 44
26:6–13	39
27:55	41
27:56	79
28:10	88
28:19	81, 88

Mark

1:30–31	33
1:31	69
5:25–34	33–34
5:35–43	34
6:43	101
7:24–30	34
8:19	101
10:2–11	18
10:2–12	43, 44
10:6	121
10:12	44
12:25	13
14:2–9	39
15:40	41, 79
16:9ff.	80

Luke

4:38–39	33
6:13	88
7:11–17	34
7:36–50	34, 39
7:37ff.	18
7:47	40
8:2–3	69, 80
10:38–42	34
13:10–17	34
16:18	43, 44
19:9	36
21:1–4	34
21:38	36
22:32	31
23:49	41
24:27	80
24:34	79, 80
24:35	83

John

2:6	101
2:7	101
2:9	101
4:1–42	34
4:22	37
4:27	18
6:13	101
6:35	83
6:53	83
6:55	83
7:36	36
7:52	36
7:53–8:11	34
8:11	18
10:3–5	83
11:1–44	34
11:2	39
11:40	83
11:44	83
12	39
12:1–8	34
20	80
20:17	88
20:31	83
21	82
21:24	36

Acts

1:3	87
1:21	81
1:21–22	86
6:2	69
8:4ff.	37
18:1–3	97
18:18–19	97
20:7	61

Romans

3:23	111
8:22	127
8:29	122
13	64
13:11	64, 87
16:1–16	66–67
16:3–5	97
16:7	67–68

1 Corinthians

1:11	56
4:5	58
4:6–9	69
7:10f.	43
7:10–12	62
7:20–22	56
7:20–24	56
9:1–14	59
9:5	59–60
9:7	60
9:8	60
9:14	60
11:5ff.	59
11:7	122
12:13	64
14:33b–40	58–59
14:35	38
15	58, 85
15:3–8	43, 83
15:3–10	87
15:5	79

16:19	97
16:22	60

2 Corinthians

3:18	122
4:4–7	122

Galatians

3:28	10, 23, 48, 62, 64, 121

Ephesians

5	11

Philippians

2:25	69, 86
4:22	56

Colossians

1:13–15	122
3:11	64

1 Thessalonians

4:15–19	51

2 Timothy

4:19	97

Philemon

2:5–8	57

Hebrews

1:3   121

1 John

1:1–4   83

Lightning Source UK Ltd.
Milton Keynes UK
UKOW06f0307110516

274009UK00003B/85/P